The
Shiitake
Way

❖

Jennifer Snyder

❖

THE BOOK PUBLISHING COMPANY
SUMMERTOWN, TENNESSEE

The Book Publishing Company
P.O. Box 99
Summertown, TN 38483

99 98 97 96   5 4 3 2

ISBN 0-913990-41-8

Cover and inside design by Barbara McNew
Cover photo by John Guider

Snyder, Jennifer, 1951-
        The Shiitake Way / by Jennifer Snyder.
                p.   cm.
        Includes index.
        ISBN 0-913990-41-8
        1. Cookery (Shiitake)   I. Title.
TX804.S64 1993
641.6'58--dc20   93-30032
                                                               CIP

Printed on recycled paper

Calculations for the nutritional analyses in this book are based on the average number of servings listed with the recipes and the average amount of an ingredient if a range is called for. Calculations are rounded up to the nearest gram. If two options for an ingredient are listed, the first one is used. Not included are fat used for frying, unless the amount is specified in the recipe, optional ingredients, or servings suggestions.

**This book is dedicated to
Marjorie Parker**

Table of Contents

Foreword

Once found only in special dishes at Chinese restaurants, shiitake mushrooms are now widely available in America and much appreciated by lovers of good food. Not long ago Americans could buy only dried shiitake, but now the fresh versions appear regularly in supermarkets. These are most welcome changes in a land that for years equated mushrooms with one, lone cultivated variety, the button mushroom of steaks, pizzas, and spinach salads. Not only are shiitake more delicious than button mushrooms, they are better for you. (See "Medicinal Properties," page 17).

Although shiitake are very good in a simple sauté, their flavor and texture make them extremely versatile. They can be the bold and central ingredient of a main dish as well as a distinctive garnish. It is worth knowing some basic information about these mushrooms in order to take advantage of their special qualities.

This book, written by two experts in the field of mushroom cultivation and mushroom cookery, will show you how to deal with shiitake most effectively, from buying and storing them to using them in a wide range of imaginative dishes. It is a great pleasure to be able to get these wonderful mushrooms, both fresh and dried, in this country today, and a great pleasure to see so many good recipes for them collected in this book.

Dr. Andrew Weil, M.D.

Introduction

Americans are familiar with shiitake as the black mushroom in Oriental cooking. Many articles have appeared describing the culinary uses and health benefits of shiitake. Today health-conscious and gourmet cooks all over the United States are cooking with shiitake, and the market is growing.

Shiitake, the most commonly accepted name for this mushroom, comes from the Japanese meaning "Shii fungus." Shiitake occur naturally on "Shii" trees, a species of beech tree, and are easily cultivated on oak species, since oaks are members of the same family. In China they are known as "Hoang-ko"[1] or "Shanku"[2] or "Hoang-mo."[3] The scientific name is *Lentinus edodes (Berk) Sing.*, having received the modern classification from Dr. Rolf Singer. A full description of the shiitake mushroom can be found in *Mushrooms and Truffles* by Dr. R. Singer and B. Harris. *L. edodes* has a dark brown to light brown cap with a somewhat reddish tinge; the younger caps are generally darker. The cap is often tufted with white scales, especially around the edges. The gills are white to off-white and may have reddish-brown spots when very old. The spore print is pure white, and the stem is likewise white, although there can be reddish-brown areas from age or bruising. When the cap is broken open, the flesh is white inside.

Shiitake is a relatively new mushroom in the United States, although it has been known for centuries in the Orient. Until 1972 the only shiitake in the U.S. were imported and dried because the live culture was not allowed into the country due to a Department of Agriculture quarantine. Apparently shiitake was confused with another species of the genus *Lentinus, Lentinus lepideus*, a fungus that is responsible for the rot in railroad ties. Since the reversal of the restrictions, there has been a steadily increasing interest in shiitake, especially among home cultivators. With the appearance of more literature in the early '80s, interest has focused on the commercial cultivation of shiitake. Estimates for the production of fresh shiitake in the U.S. in 1985 were as high as 1,200,000 pounds. This is in addition to the quantities of dried mushrooms imported from Asia, where the Japanese export to the U.S. is 2,000-3,000 metric tons annually. The earliest cultivation of shiitake in the Orient is unrecorded. It was praised as early as 199 A.D.[4] by emperors in the Kyushu district of Japan (still the area of the greatest concentration of shiitake cultivation today). At that time shiitake was gathered wild from rotten tree limbs. Methods of semi-cultivation began 250-350 years ago in China and were refined in Japan. These early methods employed a system of spore inoculation in a natural setting. Notches, called "Hodagi," were cut with hatchets on the felled tree trunks. The logs were placed near logs bearing mature shiitake mushrooms and exposed to their wind-born spores.

A refinement of this process used spores gathered on paper. The spore paper was inserted into incisions made in the logs. At the turn of the century this technique developed into a method using a suspension of spores in water as the inoculant. Spores to be used within a few days of collection were directly gathered in an emulsion. If the spores were to be stored for later use, they were collected on paper and kept completely dry and cool. The disadvantage of this method is the high degree of variability of the strains produced from spores, since the spores combine each time to produce a new strain.

At the same time the spore method became popular, another method was in use. Older logs, permeated with shiitake mycelium, were ground up and used as a source of spawn. This spawn was placed into fresh cuts in new logs. At the turn of the century, a variation of this method was developed. While both the spore method and the non-sterile spawn method were an improvement over the "wait until the wind blows" method, they suffered from the disadvantage that the mushrooms produced were of varying strains. In the 1920s, K. Kitayima introduced the modern system of sterile spawn culture—a method similar to that developed for pure culture spawn of the common button mushroom. During the 1940s in Japan, the Mori family popularized the sterile spawn method with the production of large amounts of sterilely grown spawn on wooden wedges—the true birth of the modern shiitake industry in Japan today. While this marks the beginning of commercial shiitake production, the industry did not reach large proportions until the 1960s in Japan. During this period the per capita consumption rose to the levels that exist today. The industry in Japan produces an annual revenue of over 2 billion dollars. Compare this to the revenue for the button mushroom industry in the U.S., which is about 650 million dollars. The reason for the rapid rise in consumption in Japan may be the result of the promotion of shiitake mushrooms for their health benefits. While relatively few studies have been performed in the U.S., work has been done in Japan to demonstrate both the anti-carcinogenic and the anti-cholesterol effects of shiitake. Coupled with the tradition that began in the 1950s for shiitake mushrooms to be given as gifts when traveling to friends' or relatives' houses, this had a tremendous impact on the consumption of shiitake. It is extremely common when traveling in Japan to see travelers buying large gift packs of dried mushrooms at airports and train stations.

The need for delicious recipes in the West has grown as a result of the interest in shiitake. The following recipes will open your eyes and tastes to these delicious mushrooms. To your health!

Bob Harris

Preface to the Recipes

The shiitake is a wonderful mushroom. Its flavor is hearty, its texture is smooth and firm, and there are many healthful benefits to adding shiitake to your diet. The recipes featured here are based on traditional dishes with shiitake being the featured ingredient. I have created the recipes keeping in mind people who are monitoring their fat and salt intake. Butter and salt can be added to enrich the recipes if desired. I hope you will see the shiitake mushroom as a food that is easily incorporated into your daily meals with recipes that are familiar and easy to prepare.

My eyes were opened to the many ways of using shiitake, while my dear partner in life, Bob Harris, and I led a tour of shiitake farms in Japan. The most memorable place we visited was the mushroom hotel in the province of Gunma. In the hotel lobby stands a seven foot tall wooden shiitake goddess with shiitake mushrooms extending from all parts of her body. I realized I was in for an experience of a lifetime when I was greeted by this truly magnificent statue. The hotel had shiitake tea in each room with the tea service having drawings of shiitake on the sides of the cups and tea pot. The wall fabric and the feather comforter had shiitake designs on them, as well as the robes we wore to the daily bath. Even the public hot tub had tiny pieces of shiitake floating in the water.

The first meal at the shiitake hotel was robata-style (barbecue): shiitake cooked gill side up on an open grill, heated by charcoal. This released the true essence of shiitake. We ate it simply dipped into a light soy sauce—truly god's flesh—and accompanied it with shiitake wine, of course.

The Japanese revere shiitake as a life-enhancing food and have shiitake stores near train stations filled with a myriad of products, such as soda-pop, syrup, powdered soup stock, tea, and dried shiitake, for travelers to purchase as a health giving gift when visiting family and friends

I began cooking with shiitake in 1978. Bob and I were growing shiitake on logs, and we had pounds of the mushrooms in our refrigerator, waiting to be cooked. Little did I know 14 years later, the fruits of my actions would be gathered into this book. I hope you will enjoy and experiment with shiitake mushrooms as much as I have.

Jennifer Snyder

Introduction to Shiitake Preparation

TYPES OF SHIITAKE

There are generally three grades of shiitake mushroom. In Japan these grades are called *Donko, Koko,* and *Koshin.* Donko are thick-fleshed and have rolled-in edges. Koshin are thinly fleshed with caps that tend to open up and flatten out easily. Koko grade mushrooms are between Koshin and Donko, having medium thick flesh and partially open caps. Shiitake from Asia are priced according to what grade they are, with Donko being the most expensive and Koshin being the least expensive. Shiitake grown in the U.S. are 90% fresh and graded by size only, the same as the common button mushroom. We do not place as much emphasis on grading the quality of fresh produce in this country as the Japanese do.

CLEANING

It is best to clean your mushrooms when you are ready to use them. Because shiitake are grown on wood, it is unnecessary to use water to clean them. If there happen to be particles of sawdust on the cap, just brush them off with a cloth or mushroom brush.

STEMS

When cooking with shiitake, it is best to remove and discard the stems of the mushrooms unless they happen to be unusually tender. For the most part, the stem has a tough texture—almost stringy—and has less flavor than the caps. The stem is removed by simply twisting it free from the cap and pulling, or cutting the stem with a pair of kitchen shears. It is best to leave the stems attached to the fresh mushrooms until just before they are cooked, otherwise the mushrooms will dry out. **Most of the recipes in this book require the stems to be discarded before you begin cooking the shiitake, unless otherwise noted.**

COOKING TIPS

A cast iron or enameled cast iron pan is best for cooking mushrooms. It creates an even heat and does not impart a metallic flavor to the mushrooms.

Shiitake are best cooked over lower temperatures. This way the texture is soft and smooth. Some people say the perfect shiitake melts in your mouth. When the shiitake are cooked on high heat too rapidly, their texture tends to be tough and chewy. The temperature of the burner should be low to medium-low. Shiitake will take longer than the regular button mushrooms to cook properly. As the mushroom cooks, it will exude an iridescent liquid. Taste the mushrooms and see if the texture is soft enough; it may take up to 15 minutes. **Texture is the key to the correct cooking of shiitake; always sample the food as you cook.**

Preserving - Basics Ideas

STORING FRESH SHIITAKE

Fresh shiitake mushrooms can be stored under refrigeration for as long as thirty days under ideal conditions (optimally the moisture should be about 87%) without loss of nutrition, spoilage, or significant shrinkage. In Japan the moisture of the fresh mushrooms is often between 80 and 85 percent. If the moisture content is very high, over 90 percent, the mushrooms will sweat and cause spoilage, reducing the shelf life. They should be kept in a container that allows air exchange but will not allow for too much moisture loss. Wax paper containers are the ideal. **Each hour the mushrooms are at room temperature shortens the shelf life by one day.**

FREEZING FRESH SHIITAKE

Fresh shiitake mushrooms can be frozen three ways. You can freeze fresh shiitake without processing, but only for a day or two. After that the cellular structure begins to break down. There are two methods for processing and freezing shiitake. For the first method, blanch the mushrooms by dropping them whole into boiling water for 2 minutes, then place them in freezer bags and rapidly freeze. This will inactivate the enzymes and kill any surface microorganisms that will cause spoilage. The second method is to sauté the mushrooms in oil or butter for a few minutes until the juices start to flow and then remove them from the heat. Cool the mushrooms, place them in a freezer bag, and freeze. For all of these methods it is best to cover the shiitake with some type of liquid to prevent them from getting freezer burn.

DRYING FRESH SHIITAKE

If you have too many fresh shiitake to cook all at once, you can preserve them indefinitely by drying them with any food dehydrator that has a thermostatic control. First, clean them with a mushroom brush (available in cooking stores) and remove the stems. Do not wash them in water. Lay the mushrooms on the drying trays, and set the thermostat to 105°F for one hour. Increase the temperature about 5°F each hour until the mushrooms are almost dry. During the last hour, turn the temperature up to 140°F, and dry them at this temperature for an hour. This will dramatically increase the amount of flavor in the dried mushrooms. The final product should have a moisture level of 13 percent which keeps them dry enough yet pliable. If the mushrooms are first dried in sunlight or under ultraviolet light, this helps increase the amount of Vitamin D in the dried shiitake mushrooms. To store the dried mushrooms, place them in a container that does not breath, such as a glass jar that seals or a plastic zip-lock bag.

REHYDRATING DRIED SHIITAKE

Dried shiitake are typically 13 percent water and must be rehydrated for cooking purposes. To rehydrate shiitake mushrooms, boil water in a pan, remove from heat, and soak the whole mushrooms in it for about 20 minutes or until they reach a soft texture. The rehydrated mushrooms can be used in recipes the same way fresh mushrooms are used. It is said in the Orient that the dried and rehydrated mushrooms have a stronger flavor than the fresh ones. This stronger flavor is said to be a result of the drying process in which the final stages of dehydration are done at a temperature of 140°F for one hour. It is claimed that the Donko grade of shiitake has more flavor than the others, although the differences seem to be very slight.

COOKING FRESH SHIITAKE

The most important difference between fresh mushrooms and rehydrated ones is the texture. Rehydrated mushrooms have a chewy texture after cooking, while fresh ones, if properly cooked, have a very soft texture almost like that of soft oyster or abalone. In order for freshly cooked mushrooms to achieve this soft texture, it is necessary to cook them at a low to medium-low temperature. If too high a temperature is used, the mushrooms become rubbery and tough. It takes up to 15 minutes for the mushrooms to become completely soft and fully cooked. When sautéing fresh mushrooms, the water contained in the mushrooms will be released into the skillet. This liquid is then the ideal basis for many of the sauces that are used in French, Italian, or Chinese cuisine.

EXTENDING SHIITAKE BY MIXING WITH BUTTON MUSHROOMS

When preparing larger dishes, shiitake mushrooms can be cooked together with the common, commercial button mushrooms. The flavor of shiitake is rather strong, contrasting with the button mushroom which is very mild. By combining the two mushrooms when sautéing, the flavor is distributed evenly through the mixture. I find that in many recipes I want a distinct mushroom flavor, but do not want to chew through large chunks of mushrooms to get to it, for example, in a quiche. When preparing a quiche I often use half button and half shiitake mushrooms shredding with the fine shredding blade of a food processor, a Mouli Mill, or a hand shredder. I sauté the mushrooms on medium-low heat until all of the juices flow from the mushrooms. Then I remove them from the heat and add them to the eggs for baking the quiche. Or I may add them to an omelet, scrambled eggs, stir-fried Chinese vegetables, white sauce on pasta, sautéed vegetable sauce over pasta, tomato sauce over pasta, over rice, with mixed cooked vegetables, over gluten, and just about anything else that you can think of. Once the mushrooms have been cooked until the juices flow out, they can also be sealed in a freezer bag and frozen for later use.

ALLERGIC RESPONSE TO EATING RAW SHIITAKE

It is highly recommended that shiitake mushrooms be cooked rather than eaten raw. It has been reported that some people have an allergic reaction to eating raw mushrooms, particularly children. An allergic reaction can also occur if large quantities are eaten raw at one time (i.e. 1 pound or more), especially several days in a row. The sensitivity appears as a skin rash but does not occur when eating the cooked mushrooms. This type of allergic reaction is similar to a reaction to shellfish. If one intends to eat shiitake mushrooms raw (and they actually do taste quite good raw), it is suggested that one try a small amount first to see if there is any sensitivity before increasing the amount or eating them raw for several days in a row.

Medicinal Properties

Addition of shiitake to the diet on a regular basis offers several health benefits. Like all mushrooms, shiitake are high in protein, low in fat, and devoid of cholesterol. If you cook them without adding a lot of butter, cream, oil, or cheese, you will have flavorful dishes naturally low in fat and cholesterol. Shiitake do not have natural toxins in them, as do the common button mushrooms, nor are they likely to be contaminated with residues of pesticides that are so heavily used in *Agaricus* cultivation. In addition, shiitake show some specific disease-fighting effects in tests on both animals and humans.

They have cholesterol-lowering properties, for example, due to their content of eritadenine, a compound that may help the body remove cholesterol from the bloodstream. Japanese researchers showed that adding 90 grams (about 3 ounces) of fresh shiitake to the diet every day lowered serum cholesterol by 12 percent in one week. It also counteracted rises in cholesterol caused by adding butter to the diet.

In addition, shiitake have antiviral and immunity-boosting properties that should be beneficial to people with depressed immunity from chronic viral infections and to those with high cancer risks. Of particular interest here is a compound called lentinan, a polysaccharide (large molecule made up of many subunits of sugar molecules). Lentinan is nontoxic and seems to increase activity of immune defenses against viruses and tumor cells. It is available in Japan in pure, extracted form but not in the U.S. Japanese doctors sometimes give pure lentinan to patients intravenously, and it may be more powerful by that route.

Nonetheless, eating shiitake regularly probably will help immunity, and many products containing extracts of the mushrooms are sold in health food stores, sometimes combined with other mushroom extracts or with Chinese medicinal herbs. Both fresh and dried shiitake provide lentinan.

There is little published scientific research in the West on medicinal properties of shiitake (or mushrooms in general), but even with the little we know, it would seem wise to eat these fruits of the earth whenever they are available.

Even if shiitake had no special health benefits, their delicious flavor and appealing texture would recommend them as food.

Dr. Andrew Weil, M.D.

❖ Basic Preparation ❖

Duxelles

Yields 1-2 ounces

Duxelles is a French term for processing large amounts of fresh mushrooms into a concentrate. The name was originated by La Varenne, the head chef for Louis Chalon du Bled, Marquis d'Uxelles. His recipes were published in 1651.

> 1 pound mushrooms, shredded or processed in a juicer
> 1 sheet of cheesecloth, 24" x 12", folded in half
> 2 tablespoons olive oil
> 4 shallots, finely chopped
> 1 cup Madeira wine

Place the shredded mushrooms in a double layer of cheesecloth, and squeeze to extract as much liquid as possible. Set the mushroom mash aside. Keep the mushroom liquid for soups or sauces.

In a cast iron skillet over low heat, add 1 tablespoon oil and the mushroom mash. Cook slowly, stirring every 10 minutes. Cook the Duxelles for approximately 1 hour, until it is reduced to a dark color, but not burnt. The liquid evaporates leaving a very concentrated mushroom flavor. Set aside.

In a sauté pan, cook the shallots in 1 tablespoon oil over medium heat until transparent. Add the Madeira and cook down the liquid to ½ cup. Add to the Duxelles.

Duxelles will keep in the refrigerator 3-4 weeks. For long term storage, place in freezer bags, adding a pinch of ascorbic acid (powdered Vitamin C) as a preservative. This is an excellent way to process older, less esthetic mushrooms, or a large quantity of mushrooms, since it reduces the bulk of the mushrooms by about 15 fold.

Duxelles are excellent as a soup stock concentrate, as an addition to red or white sauces to enhance the flavor, in combination with ricotta cheese for raviolis, alone as a pâté, or combined 50/50 with kefir cheese on toast.

Freezing Duxelles

Freeze the Duxelles in ice-cube trays. Remove the cubes when frozen, and place in a sealed plastic bag. They will last up to 6 months. This way the whole block of Duxelles does not need to be defrosted when you only need a little bit for flavoring soup, sauces, stuffing ravioli, or creating a Duxelles spread.

Shiitake Stock

Makes approximately 7 cups of stock.

This stock has a full bodied flavor and is excellent frozen for future use.

1½ ounces dried shiitake, stems removed

½ pound fresh shiitake (1⅓ cups), stems removed, sliced

1 large leek, sliced

2 celery stalks, chopped

2 bay leaves

½ teaspoon dried sage

4 cloves garlic, chopped

⅓ cup parsley, chopped

1 teaspoon low-sodium soy sauce

9 cups water

Combine all ingredients in a heavy-bottomed soup pot and bring to a boil. Cover and simmer for 45 minutes. Strain the stock and discard all the vegetables except the mushrooms. Save the mushrooms for other dishes. Continue to reduce the stock at a simmer for 15 minutes or more to intensify the flavor.

Shiitake Extract

Makes 1½ cups

An excellent way to create a very concentrated mushroom flavor for soups and sauces.

5 ounces fresh or reconstituted shiitake, stems removed
3 cups water
1 tablespoon low-sodium soy sauce
pinch of sugar

In a large saucepan, bring water, mushrooms, soy sauce, and sugar to a boil. Reduce the heat and simmer 30 minutes, uncovered.

Remove the mushrooms, slice, and add to the extract. The extract may be stored in a covered jar in the refrigerator for one week.

Shiitake Puree

The puree can be used as a filling for baby zucchini, scooped out tomatoes, or puff pastry.

Yield 2-3 cups

1 tablespoon olive oil
1 onion, chopped
1 pound fresh or reconstituted shiitake (2⅔ cups), chopped
1 tablespoon low-sodium soy sauce
4 tablespoons water

In a sauté pan, heat the oil, add the onions, and sauté until the onions become transparent. Add the mushrooms and continue to cook over a medium heat for 15-20 minutes. Add soy sauce. Transfer the mixture into a blender or food processor, and add the water to help the mixture blend easily. More water may be added if necessary. Allow to cool and store in a refrigerator.

Shiitake Butter

Makes 1 cup

This is an easy way to add mushroom flavor to a dish. It is very good served on potatoes, pasta, and hearty breads. When sautéing, use Shiitake Butter instead of plain butter to enhance the flavor of a dish.

½ cup butter
½ cup Shiitake Puree

Have the butter and Shiitake Puree at room temperature. In a large bowl, blend both ingredients. The Shiitake Butter will keep refrigerated for a few weeks or frozen for six months.

Shiitake Powder

Shiitake powder can be added to soups, pasta, or anywhere you would like the addition of the subtle shiitake flavor.

Make sure the shiitake are completely dried. They should crack at the touch and not bend. If they are a little soft, place them in an oven set to 300°F until they crack to the touch.

Place the dried shiitake in an electric grinder, blender, or food processor, and process to a fine powder. Store in a tightly sealed jar.

Sautéed Shredded Shiitake

*A food processor is the simplest tool to use to shred these mushrooms. If you don't
have one, simply shred by hand.*

> 1 tablespoon olive oil
> 1 pound fresh shiitake (2⅔ cups), shredded
> flavorings to taste

In a cast iron skillet, heat the olive oil over medium-low heat. Add the
mushrooms and stir. The mixture will create quite a bit of liquid. Sauté about
15-20 minutes, until most of the liquid has evaporated.

Suggested flavorings are shallots, pepper, nutmeg, or soy sauce.

Add Shredded Shiitake to cooked rice, an uncooked soufflé, or pasta. The
shiitake flavor suspends itself throughout the mixture beautifully.

❖ # Appetizers ❖

Marinated Shiitake with Herbs

Serves 4 - 6

2 tablespoons olive oil

3 tablespoons balsamic vinegar or red wine vinegar

3 cloves garlic, sliced

1 teaspoon low-sodium soy sauce

½ teaspoon freshly ground pepper

3 tablespoons fresh parsley, chopped

pinch of fresh herbs (oregano, rosemary, marjoram, or savory)

2 tablespoons Madeira wine

½ pound fresh shiitake (1⅓ cups), stems removed, cut in half or
    quarters if large

In a large saucepan, combine all the ingredients except the shiitake, bring to a boil, and simmer for 5 minutes. Add the shiitake and simmer for 20 minutes. Remove the saucepan from the heat, and cool the shiitake in the liquid. Drain and serve on a plate with bite-sized, thinly sliced French bread.

Per Serving: Calories: 79, Protein: 1 gm., Fat: 6 gm., Carbohydrates: 5 gm.

Mushroom Pâté

Makes about 16 appetizers

2 tablespoons olive oil
2 medium red onions, finely chopped
⅓ cup celery, chopped
1 pound fresh shiitake (2⅔ cups), stems removed, chopped
2 eggs, lightly beaten
3 ounces low-fat cream cheese
½ teaspoon dried basil
½ teaspoon rosemary
½ teaspoon oregano
½ teaspoon pepper
1 cup bread crumbs, finely ground
1 bunch cilantro or parsley for garnish

Preheat oven to 325°F. In a large frying pan, heat the oil. Sauté onions and celery; cook for 2 minutes. Add mushrooms and sauté for 15 minutes on medium heat, then set aside. In a large bowl, combine eggs, cream cheese, basil, rosemary, oregano, and pepper. Add mushroom mixture and bread crumbs, and mix well. Turn onto an oiled 9" x 5" loaf pan. Cover with foil and bake for 1 hour. Cool and refrigerate.

To serve, turn out of the pan and slice. Garnish with cilantro or parsley.

Per Slice: Calories: 90, Protein: 3 gm., Fat: 3 gm., Carbohydrates: 9 gm.

Shiitake Caponata

Serves 10-12

2 tablespoons olive oil

2 medium onions, chopped

1 stalk celery, chopped

3 green peppers, chopped

3 medium eggplants, cut into ¾-inch cubes, unpeeled

1 pound fresh shiitake (2⅔ cups), stems removed, chopped

½ cup wine vinegar

1 teaspoon red pepper, powder or crushed

1 tablespoon sugar

1 teaspoon low-sodium soy sauce

1 (28-ounce) can tomatoes, drained and chopped

½ cup green olives, chopped

½ cup black olives, chopped

In a large sauté pan, heat the oil, add onions, celery, and peppers, and cook on medium heat for 10 minutes, until the onions are transparent. Add the eggplant and mushrooms, and sauté for 10 minutes. Add the vinegar, red pepper, sugar, soy sauce, and tomatoes, and cook until the eggplant is tender. Add the olives and let the mixture stand for half an hour. Serve warm or chill and serve cold with crackers.

Per Serving: Calories: 132, Protein: 3 gm., Fat: 5 gm., Carbohydrates: 21 gm.

Cold Japanese Style Marinated Shiitake

Serves 4 - 6

1 tablespoon light brown sugar

½ cup low-sodium soy sauce

½ cup sake or dry sherry

½ pound fresh shiitake (1⅓ cups), stems removed, cut in half if large

1 teaspoon roasted (dark) sesame oil

paper-thin slices of scallion for garnish

In a saucepan, dissolve sugar in soy sauce and sake. Add mushrooms and bring to boil, mixing well. Lower to medium heat and cook uncovered, stirring occasionally, until liquid is almost all evaporated. Toss mushrooms to glaze in remaining liquid, being careful to avoid burning. Remove from heat. Cool, then chill mushrooms in refrigerator. Sprinkle with drops of sesame oil and scallion slices before serving.

Per Serving: Calories: 95, Protein: 4 gm., Fat: 1 gm., Carbohydrates: 11 gm.

Andrew Weil

Mushroom Tartlets

Makes 20 tartlets

PASTRY:
9 ounces fat-free cream cheese
½ cup butter
1½ cups whole wheat pastry flour

FILLING:
1-2 tablespoons oil
½ cup onion, finely chopped
½ pound fresh or reconstituted shiitake (1⅓ cups), stems removed, finely chopped
¼ cup celery, chopped
pinch of salt
freshly ground black pepper
2 tablespoons flour
¼ cup soy or dairy sour cream or non-fat yogurt

Make sure the cream cheese and butter are at room temperature. Mix together thoroughly. Work in the flour with a pastry blender until completely incorporated, and chill for at least 30 minutes.

In a heavy frying pan, heat the oil and brown the onions over low heat, approximately 10 minutes. Add the shiitake and celery, and cook, stirring, for 3 to 4 minutes. Taste the mixture and season with salt and pepper. Stir in the flour, then the cream, and cook slowly until thickened. Set aside.

Preheat oven to 450°F. Roll the chilled dough to ⅛-inch thickness on a lightly floured board, and cut into rounds with a 3-inch biscuit cutter. Place a teaspoon of mushroom filling on each circle, and fold the dough over the filling. Press the edges together with a fork, and prick the tops to allow steam to escape. Place on an ungreased baking sheet, and bake for 15 minutes or until lightly browned. Serve hot.

Per Tartlet: Calories: 127, Protein: 3 gm., Fat: 9 gm., Carbohydrates: 9 gm.

Grilled Shiitake

Serves 4-6

16 large fresh shiitake, stems removed
4 tablespoons low-sodium soy sauce
4 tablespoons lemon juice
1 tablespoon mirin
2 tablespoons scallions, finely chopped
¼ teaspoon chili powder or to taste

Place mushrooms stem side up on hot charcoal grill, and cook 2 or 3 minutes. Turn mushrooms over and cook 2 or 3 minutes more. For a dipping sauce, combine soy sauce, lemon juice, mirin, chopped scallions, and chili powder. Serve mushrooms immediately with sauce.

Per Serving: Calories: 54, Protein: 3 gm., Fat: 0 gm., Carbohydrates: 10 gm.

K.C. Mushroom Petit Fours

Makes 20 sandwiches

20 slices whole grain bread, thinly sliced

3 tablespoons onion, grated

2½ teaspoons canola oil

¾ pound fresh shiitake (2 cups), stems removed, finely chopped

2 tablespoons flour

½ teaspoon Tabasco sauce

1 teaspoon low-sodium soy sauce

pinch of pepper to taste

½ cup soy or dairy milk

With a 2-inch biscuit cutter, cut each slice of bread into 2 rounds. Sauté onion in 2 teaspoons oil. Add mushrooms and cook until liquid has evaporated. Add flour and stir. Add Tabasco sauce, soy sauce, pepper, and milk. Cook until thick.

Spread 2 tablespoons of the mushroom mixture on each round of bread. Top with another round of bread.

Coat a medium-hot grill with a thin layer of canola oil, and brown the sandwiches until crisp, about 1 minute for each side. Place on a piece of paper towel. Keep warm in a low oven until all sandwiches are ready to serve.

Per Sandwich: Calories: 90, Protein: 4 gm., Fat: 3 gm., Carbohydrates: 14 gm.

Stuffed Mushrooms with Nuts

Serves 6

1½ pounds fresh medium shiitake (4 cups), caps slightly closed
3 tablespoons unsalted butter, room temperature
¼ cup pecans, minced
¼ cup walnuts, minced
¼ cup pine nuts, minced
2 tablespoons shallots or scallions, minced
2 tablespoons fresh parsley, minced
1 teaspoon low-sodium soy sauce
¼ teaspoon thyme
¼ teaspoon marjoram
⅛ teaspoon freshly ground black pepper
⅛ teaspoon ground mace or nutmeg
2 tablespoons Madeira
⅓ cup bread crumbs
1½ cups soy or low-fat dairy milk

Preheat oven to 300°F. Remove mushroom stems from the caps and set aside.

Combine the rest of the ingredients, except for the milk. Stuff each mushroom cap with the mixture, packing it in lightly and mounding it in the center. Arrange the mushrooms in a shallow, ungreased baking pan or au gratin dish. Pour the milk around the mushrooms, about two-thirds of the way up their sides. Bake, uncovered, basting every 10 to 15 minutes for about 1 hour or until the mushrooms are tender and the filling is lightly browned.

If you've baked the mushrooms in an au gratin dish, serve them directly from the dish.

Per Serving: Calories: 355, Protein: 6 gm., Fat: 26 gm., Carbohydrates: 1 gm.

Shiitake Roll Appetizers

Makes 80 appetizers

2 tablespoons olive oil

1 small onion, minced

1 pound fresh shiitake (2⅔ cups), stems removed, finely chopped

6 tablespoons flour

1 teaspoon low-sodium soy sauce

2 cups low-fat milk

2 teaspoons lemon juice

1 loaf sliced white sandwich bread (crusts removed)

4 tablespoons canola oil

Preheat oven to 400°F. In a large skillet, heat the oil, add the onions, and cook until soft. Add the mushrooms, and cook for 15-20 minutes on medium-low. Remove from heat, add flour and soy sauce, and blend well. Stir in milk. Cook over low heat, stirring constantly, until thick. Add lemon juice and cool.

Roll the bread slices with a rolling pin until they are as thin as pastry. Spread filling on each slice, enough to cover. Roll up bread to form a long roll. Place on a cookie sheet, seam side down, and refrigerate for a few hours. Cut each roll into 3 segments, and brush with oil. Bake for 15 minutes until nicely brown.

Per Roll: Calories: 39, Protein: 1 gm., Fat: 1 gm., Carbohydrates: 5 gm.

Mushroom Croutons

Excellent with soup.

1 tablespoon canola oil

3 ounces fresh or reconstituted shiitake (½ cup), stems removed, minced

2 teaspoons fresh parsley, minced

1 clove garlic, minced

8 slices bread

In a small bowl mix, oil, mushrooms, parsley, and garlic.

Toast bread under broiler on one side. Remove from oven and spread the mushrooms on the untoasted side. Return to oven and toast bread slices until golden brown.

Serve immediately.

Per ⅛ recipe: Calories: 92, Protein: 3 gm., Fat: 3 gm., Carbohydrates: 13 gm.

Piroshki

Makes fifty 2-inch piroshki

DOUGH:
2 cups sifted flour
½ pound margarine
6 tablespoons sour cream

FILLING:
1 tablespoon canola oil
1 medium onion, chopped
6-8 small fresh shiitake, stems removed, chopped
½ cup mashed potatoes
1 egg, separated
1 teaspoon low-sodium soy sauce
½ teaspoon pepper
pinch of nutmeg

DOUGH:

Sift the flour. Cut margarine into pieces, add to flour, and work in with fingertips until it forms a coarse meal. Place in a large bowl, and add sour cream. Mix until flour forms a ball; divide into two parts, wrap in wax paper, and refrigerate two hours or overnight.

FILLING:

In a large sauté pan, heat the oil, add the onions, and sauté over low heat until soft. Add the shiitake, and sauté until tender, about 12 minutes. Add the potatoes, mix, and remove from heat. Add slightly beaten egg yolk, soy sauce, pepper, and nutmeg.

Lightly flour board and rolling pin. Press the ball of dough down with the palm of the hand, and roll as thinly as possible. Cut with a 2" round cookie cutter. Paint the edges of each round with beaten egg white. Fill with ½ teaspoon filling, fold into a half moon shape, and seal the edges with a fork.

Preheat oven to 450°F. Place on a baking sheet, and brush tops with the egg yolks. Bake for 15 minutes or until brown.

Per Piroshki: Calories: 60, Protein: 1 gm., Fat: 5 gm., Carbohydrates: 4 gm.

Marinated Shiitake

Yield: approximately 3 quarts

3 cups balsamic vinegar
½ teaspoon peppercorns
several sprigs fresh parsley
3 bay leaves
1 tablespoon celery seed
4 medium onions, sliced
3 pounds fresh shiitake (8 cups), stems removed
2 quarts water
1 tablespoon low-sodium soy sauce
1 cup olive oil

In a large saucepan, mix together vinegar, peppercorns, parsley, bay leaves, celery seed, and a few slices of the onion.

Bring to a boil and simmer for 10 minutes. Set aside.

Leave the small shiitake whole, and cut the large ones into bite-sized portions. In a very large soup pot, cover the shiitake and remaining sliced onions with water and soy sauce. Bring to a boil, simmer for 5 minutes, and drain. Pour the vinegar mixture over the shiitake and onions, and cool. Add the olive oil. Place in a tightly covered jar, and shake well. Refrigerate at least 24 hours, shaking occasionally. Drain before serving.

Per ¼ cup shiitake: Calories: 65, Protein: 1 gm., Fat: 5 gm., Carbohydrates: 5 gm.

❖ · # Sauces · ❖

Supreme Shiitake Sauce

Serves 4

2½ tablespoons canola oil

1 cup onion, chopped

6 cloves garlic, minced

1 pound tofu, crumbled

½ cup green pepper, chopped

¼ cup celery, chopped

2 (8-ounce) cans tomato sauce

1 (6-ounce) can tomato paste

1 cup water

1 bay leaf

2 tablespoons fresh parsley, chopped

1 tablespoon oregano

1 tablespoon basil

1 teaspoon low-sodium soy sauce

pinch of sugar

1½ teaspoons pepper, freshly ground

¼ pound fresh or reconstituted shiitake (⅔ cup), stems removed, sliced

Heat 2 tablespoons oil in a heavy saucepan, and add onion, garlic, and tofu. Fry until tofu is browned, stirring constantly. Add green pepper and celery. Sauté 10 minutes. Add the rest of the ingredients except fresh shiitake. Simmer 1 hour.

In a sauté pan, heat ½ tablespoon oil, and sauté fresh shiitake for 10 minutes. Set aside.

Remove bay leaf from sauce. Add shiitake and continue cooking sauce for 15 minutes. Can be served over pasta with a sprinkling of grated Parmesan cheese, if desired.

Variation: Serve over rice or Shiitake Nut and Cheese Loaf, page 84.

Per Serving: Calories: 253, Protein: 11 gm., Fat: 10 gm., Carbohydrates: 27 gm.

Mushroom Sauce for Pasta

Serves 4 as a side dish

¾ pound fresh or reconstituted shiitake (2 cups), stems removed,
    sliced
1 tablespoon olive oil
¼ cup onion, minced
1 large clove garlic, minced
¼ cup Parmesan cheese, freshly grated
½ cup half-and-half or milk

Thinly slice the mushrooms. Set aside.

In a large skillet, heat the oil and add the onion and garlic. Cook until they are soft, but not brown. Add the shiitake, raise the heat a little, and cook 10 minutes longer. Add a little water or vegetable stock to keep the mushrooms from sticking. They should end up being very soft and the liquid translucent.

Remove mushrooms from the heat. Stir in the Parmesan cheese and half-and-half or milk, and serve over hot pasta.

(For a lighter sauce you can replace the half-and-half with low-fat milk or soymilk.)

Per Serving: Calories: 115, Protein: 5 gm., Fat: 5 gm., Carbohydrates: 11 gm.

Dark Shiitake Sauce

Makes 2 cups

1 ounce dried shiitake
3 cups water
pinch of sugar
1 tablespoon low-sodium soy sauce
1 tablespoon arrowroot or cornstarch mixed with ¼ cup water

In a saucepan, bring all the ingredients to a boil except the arrowroot. Reduce heat and simmer 30 minutes.

Add the arrowroot and water mixture, stir until thickened, and serve immediately.

Per ¼ cup: Calories: 19, Protein: 1 gm., Fat: 0 gm., Carbohydrates: 4 gm.

Creamy Shiitake Sauce

Makes 3 cups

1 tablespoon canola oil
2 tablespoons flour
3 cups Shiitake Stock (page 21)
1 tablespoon tomato paste
salt and freshly ground black pepper to taste
¼ cup half-and-half or soymilk (optional)

In a saucepan, heat the oil over low heat, add the flour, stir for a few minutes, and remove from heat. Heat the Shiitake Stock and add to the flour. Stir in the tomato paste and salt and pepper. Add half-and-half or soymilk, if desired. Cook for 15-20 minutes.

Try serving these sauces over steamed vegetables, grains, pasta, potatoes, etc.

Per ¼ cup: Calories: 20 gm., Protein: 0 gm., Fat: 1 gm., Carbohydrates: 2 gm.,

Cheese Sauce with Shiitake

Makes 2 cups

1 cup low-fat cottage cheese
⅓ cup Shiitake Stock (page 21)
1 teaspoon Worcestershire sauce
1 medium onion, minced
¼ pound fresh shiitake (⅔ cup), stems removed, thinly sliced
1 teaspoon canola oil
1 clove garlic, minced

In a food processor or blender, blend the cottage cheese, Shiitake Stock, and Worcestershire sauce until smooth. Set aside.

In a large frying pan, sauté the onions and shiitake in oil over medium-low heat for 10-15 minutes, stirring frequently. Add the garlic and stir for 1 minute. Remove the pan from the heat, and stir in the cottage cheese mixture. Warm over medium-low heat.

Per ¼ cup: Calories: 39, Protein: 4 gm., Fat: 0 gm., Carbohydrates: 4 gm.

Shiitake Tempura Dipping Sauce

Makes 1 ¼ cups

2 tablespoons mirin
1 cup Shiitake Stock (page 21)
2 tablespoons low-sodium soy sauce

In a saucepan, heat together mirin, shiitake stock, and soy sauce.
Cool and serve in small dishes as a dipping sauce for tempura.

Per 1 tablespoon: Calories: 50, Protein: 0 gm., Fat: 0 gm., Carbohydrates: 1 gm.

Shiitake Mushrooms in Sour Cream

Serves 4

1 tablespoon canola oil

1 medium onion, finely chopped

1 pound fresh or reconstituted shiitake (2⅔ cups), stems removed, sliced

¼ cup fresh bread crumbs

1 teaspoon low-sodium soy sauce

pepper to taste

¾ cup soy or dairy sour cream

1 tablespoon fresh parsley, chopped

Heat oil in a large skillet. Add onion and sauté until transparent.

Add shiitake and cook 10 minutes, stirring occasionally. Sprinkle bread crumbs over mushroom mixture, and stir in. Season with soy sauce and pepper. Remove pan from heat and gently stir in sour cream. Spoon into individual serving dishes, and garnish with parsley.

Can be served on toasted rounds of bread.

Per Serving: Calories: 146, Protein: 5 gm., Fat: 4 gm., Carbohydrates: 21 gm.

Shiitake Marinade
à la Grecque

1 cup olive oil, to cover shiitake
3 large lemons, juiced
12 large fresh shiitake

In a medium bowl, add the lemon juice to the olive oil, and mix.

Add the shiitake to the marinade stirring to cover. Allow to sit overnight. The next day, bring the shiitake to a boil, then remove from the heat and cool. Remove shiitake from marinade, and serve as a cold hors d'oeuvre, with a little lemon juice added at the last moment.

Per Mushroom: Calories: 59, Protein: 1 gm., Fat: 4 gm., Carbohydrates: 4 gm.

❖ Soups ❖

Chinese Mushroom Soup

Serves 4-6

12 dried shiitake mushrooms
3 cups Shiitake Stock (page 21)
2 (5-inch) pieces lemon grass (available in Asian grocery stores)
4 thin slices gingerroot, plus ½ teaspoon gingerroot, chopped
4 cilantro springs

pinch of sugar
4 green onions, chopped
2 tablespoons low-sodium soy sauce
3 tablespoons rice wine

Put mushrooms in a bowl. Add just enough boiling water to cover, and set aside for 30 minutes. Remove the shiitake and reserve liquid, discarding any gritty residue left in the bottom of the bowl. Cut stems from shiitake and discard, cutting the remaining mushrooms into quarters.

In a large saucepan, bring Shiitake Stock, mushroom soaking liquid, lemon grass, gingerroot slices, and cilantro to a boil. Reduce heat, cover, and simmer 30 minutes. Remove the lemon grass, gingerroot slices, and cilantro.

Return stock to pan and add mushrooms, chopped ginger, and remaining ingredients. Bring to a boil, reduce heat, cover, and simmer a few minutes longer. Adjust seasoning to taste and serve.

Per Serving: Calories: 56, Protein: 3 gm., Fat: 0 gm., Carbohydrates: 9 gm.

Cream of Mushroom Soup

Serves 6

- 3 tablespoons canola oil
- 1 pound fresh or reconstituted shiitake (2⅔ cups), stems removed, coarsely chopped
- 1 medium yellow onion, peeled and chopped
- 3 tablespoons flour
- ⅛ teaspoon ground nutmeg
- 3 cups milk or plain soymilk
- 1¾ cups Shiitake Stock (page 21)
- 1 tablespoon lemon juice
- Salt and freshly ground black pepper to taste

In a medium soup pot, heat 1 tablespoon oil. Sauté mushrooms and onions for 10 to 15 minutes over moderate heat, stirring frequently, until onions are lightly browned and all mushroom juices have evaporated.

In a medium saucepan, heat 2 tablespoons oil over moderate heat, and blend in flour and nutmeg to make a smooth paste. Cook and stir for 2-3 minutes. Add milk and stir for 3-5 minutes, until the sauce is thick and smooth and no raw flour taste remains. Remove pan from heat and set aside.

When mushrooms and onions are lightly browned, add Shiitake Stock. Simmer mixture, uncovered, for 5 minutes. Puree mushrooms in a food processor fitted with the metal chopping blade for 60 seconds nonstop. Return mushroom puree to the pot. Blend in milk or soymilk mixture, and set the pot over low heat. Mix in lemon juice, salt, and pepper. Bring the soup slowly to serving temperature, stirring frequently. If the soup seems too thick, add additional milk. Serve hot, garnished with a few mushroom slices browned in oil. Or chill soup and serve with a lemon slice and watercress floating on top.

Per Serving: Calories: 163, Protein: 5 gm., Fat: 10 gm., Carbohydrates: 15 gm.

Four Mushroom Sauce and Soba Noodles

Serves 4

¼ pound oyster mushrooms

¼ pound fresh or reconstituted shiitake (⅔ cup), stems removed

¼ pound chanterelles

¼ pound white button mushrooms

2 tablespoons canola oil

2 tablespoons low-sodium soy sauce

2 tablespoons sake

½ cup dashi stock*

3 quarts water

1 pound mushroom-flavored or regular soba (buckwheat noodles)

1 package enoki mushrooms, for garnish

2 tablespoons fresh parsley, chopped

Cut all mushrooms (except enoki garnish) into bite-sized pieces. In a large skillet, heat the oil. When oil is hot, add mushrooms except enoki, and sauté over medium-high heat for a few minutes. Add soy sauce, sake, and dashi stock, reduce heat to low, cover, and cook 15 minutes. For a stronger taste, add more dashi stock to taste.

In a 4-quart pot, bring water to a boil. Add soba, stir, and cook until al dente. Drain in a colander and transfer to a serving bowl. Pour mushroom sauce over the soba. Garnish with enoki tops and chopped parsley.

* Soba and dried dashi are available in Asian grocery stores. To make dashi stock use ½ teaspoon dried dashi to 1 cup water.

Per Serving: Calories: 282, Protein: 12 gm., Fat: 8 gm., Carbohydrates: 39 gm.

❖ Egg Recipes ❖

Shiitake Soufflé

Serves 4

½ pound fresh shiitake (1⅓ cups), stems removed, shredded
1 tablespoon extra virgin olive oil
2 tablespoons butter
¼ cup flour
1 cup milk
pinch of salt
½ cup Parmesan cheese, grated
4 large egg yolks, beaten until light
4 large egg whites

In a sauté pan, heat 1 tablespoon oil, add shiitake, and sauté for 15 minutes, over medium heat, until most of the liquid has evaporated, and set aside.

In a saucepan, over low heat, melt butter and blend in the flour. Cook for 5 minutes, stirring constantly. Add the milk slowly and stir until thick and smooth. Add a pinch of salt, cheese, and shiitake. Remove from heat and add egg yolks. Preheat the oven to 325°F. Just before baking, beat 4 egg whites until stiff but not dry and fold into the egg yolk mixture. Pour mixture into a greased 1½-quart soufflé dish. Place soufflé dish in a pan of hot water, and bake 30-45 minutes, until well risen, browned, and firm on top.

Serve immediately.

Per Serving: Calories: 301, Protein: 17 gm., Fat: 17 gm., Carbohydrates: 14 gm.

Shiitake Omelet

Serves 4

1 teaspoon canola oil

¼ pound fresh shiitake (⅔ cup), stems removed, thinly sliced

2 green onions, chopped fine

6 eggs, lightly beaten

2 tablespoons milk

In a sauté pan, heat ½ teaspoon oil over medium heat, and sauté shiitake. Cook until liquid has evaporated, about 15 minutes. Add the green onions, and cook for 5 minutes. Set aside.

Beat the eggs and milk together with a fork until blended. In an omelette pan or sauté pan, heat ½ teaspoon oil over medium heat. Add egg mixture and let cook for about 7 seconds, then begin to swirl the egg mixture in the pan. Using a spatula take the edge of the mixture and pull it toward the center to allow the uncooked egg mixture to flow toward the edge of the pan and cook.

When the eggs begin to set up, about a minute or less, add sautéed shiitake and onions. Fold in half and serve.

Per Serving: Calories: 171, Protein: 14 gm., Fat: 10 gm., Carbohydrates: 4 gm.

Mushroom and Egg Sandwiches

Makes 4 to 6 sandwiches

1 ¼ tablespoons canola oil

1 pound fresh shiitake (1⅓ cups), stems removed, thinly sliced

¼ cup green onions, sliced

1½ tablespoons chives, chopped

¼ teaspoon tarragon leaves, crumbled

salt and freshly ground black pepper to taste

6 eggs, lightly beaten

8-12 slices whole grain bread

In a large skillet, heat 1 tablespoon oil and sauté the mushrooms on medium-low until soft and the liquid is evaporated, about 15 minutes. Set aside.

In the same skillet, heat ¼ teaspoon oil, and add green onions, chives, tarragon, and salt and black pepper to taste. Sauté 2 minutes. Add eggs, cooking and stirring very gently until eggs begin to firm up. Stir in sautéed mushrooms and heat only until hot.

Divide mushroom-egg filling over 6 bread slices; top with remaining bread slices, securing with toothpicks if necessary. Toast sandwiches under broiler or grill in skillet, turning once.

Per Sandwich: Calories: 361, Protein: 17 gm., Fat: 16 gm., Carbohydrates: 35 gm.

Cheese and Mushroom Omelet

Serves 2

½ cup low-fat cottage cheese
2 fresh shiitake mushrooms, stems removed, thinly sliced
2 tablespoons onion, minced
4 eggs
salt and freshly ground pepper to taste
1 tablespoon canola oil
3 tablespoons cheddar cheese, shredded

Mix cottage cheese, mushrooms, and onions. Set aside.

Beat eggs, salt, and pepper in a small bowl. Heat a 10-inch, heavy frying pan for 30 seconds, and add oil. Pour in egg mixture.

Cook at medium-low heat. Loosen omelet around edges with a fork so eggs will seep underneath and cook. Shake pan back and forth until omelet is firm on the bottom but soft on top. Turn off heat.

Remove pan from stove. Sprinkle cheddar cheese on omelet.

Place cottage cheese mixture in a line down the center of the omelet. Fold over half of the omelet. Roll over onto a heated dish, and garnish with parsley, if desired.

Per Serving: Calories: 252, Protein: 19 gm., Fat: 16 gm., Carbohydrates: 6 gm.

Eggs and Shiitake

Serves 4

6 large eggs
1 tablespoon milk
1 teaspoon oil
¼ pound firm tofu
1 small onion, sliced
¼ pound fresh shiitake (⅔ cup), stems removed, sliced
salt and freshly ground black pepper to taste

Whisk eggs and milk in a medium bowl. Set aside.

Preheat a skillet over medium heat. Add oil and heat.

Crumble tofu and fry in skillet until browned, about 8-10 minutes, stirring occasionally. Remove tofu from skillet and place on a paper towel.

Using the same pan, sauté sliced onion until transparent. Add shiitake to onions in skillet, and cook 10 minutes until soft and the juice exudes from the mushrooms. Be sure not to use too high a heat or the mushrooms will become tough. Add salt and pepper to taste.

Add fried tofu to the shiitake and onions, and sauté over medium heat. Add the well-beaten eggs and gently toss with a spatula.

Do not stir the eggs constantly. Allow them to cook undisturbed for 30 seconds, then gently toss them over. Repeat until eggs are at the desired consistency.

Per Serving: Calories: 194, Protein: 16 gm., Fat: 11 gm., Carbohydrates: 5 gm.

Bob Harris

Custard with Shiitake

Serves 4

½ pound soft tofu
2 eggs, lightly beaten
1½ cups Shiitake Stock (page 21)
pinch of salt
1 dash of mirin
40 pine nuts
8 fresh or reconstituted shiitake
1 sheet nori seaweed, crumbled
8 spinach leaves, cut into thin strips

Puree tofu in a food processor. In a large bowl, mix the tofu, eggs, Shiitake Stock, salt, and mirin.

In a steamer, heat water over high heat. Divide the tofu-egg mixture evenly among four custard cups. Sprinkle the pine nuts over the top of the custard mixture with two shiitake caps on top of each cup. Place the uncovered custard cups in the steamer, setting the cups in the simmering water. The water should come three-quarters of the way up the sides of the cups. The lid of the steamer should be wrapped in a towel, so that moisture does not drip into the custard. Cook over high heat for 4 minutes. Reduce heat, cover steamer only three-quarters of the way with the lid, and steam for 10 minutes. Place the seaweed and spinach atop the custard, cover, and steam another 5 minutes.

The custard is done when a toothpick inserted in the center comes out clean. The custard will separate if overcooked.

Can be served hot or cold.

Per Serving: Calories: 123, Protein: 10 gm., Fat: 6 gm., Carbohydrates: 7 gm.

❖ Sandwiches ❖

Pita Mushroom Sandwich

Serves 1

1 pita bread
mayonnaise
1 slice Monterey Jack cheese
1 slice sharp cheddar cheese
2 fresh shiitake, stems removed, thinly sliced
3 avocado slices
1 tablespoon sunflower seeds (optional)
1 slice tomato
1 slice red onion
fresh alfalfa sprouts

Preheat oven to 350°F. Cut pita bread in half and open pockets. Spread a dab of mayonnaise inside each half.

Fill with above ingredients except sprouts. Wrap in aluminum foil.

Heat in oven for 10 minutes. Open foil and top with sprouts.

Per Serving: Calories: 313, Protein: 11 gm., Fat: 12 gm., Carbohydrates: 37 gm.

Shiitake Tofu Burger

Serves 1

1 commercial tofu burger
1 teaspoon olive oil
1 slice onion
4 fresh shiitake, stems removed, sliced
pinch of pepper
1 whole wheat bun

Cook tofu burger according to package directions.

In a cast iron skillet, heat oil. Sauté sliced onion until transparent. Add sliced shiitake and pepper to taste. Cook on medium to low heat for 10 minutes, until the mushrooms are tender and soft and the juice has exuded from the mushrooms.

Top the burger with the mushrooms and onions, and serve on a bun.

Per Serving: Calories: 294, Protein: 15 gm., Fat: 11 gm., Carbohydrates: 34 gm.

Bob Harris

❖ Pasta and Grains ❖

Shiitake Pasta

Makes 2 pounds - Serves 6

1 ounce dried shiitake

1½ cups semolina flour

1½ cups unbleached flour

2 tablespoons olive oil

4 large eggs

4 large egg yolks

4 quarts water

Process the dried mushrooms to a powder in an electric coffee-herb grinder. Combine the shiitake powder with the flour. Insert the metal blade attachment in a food processor, and add half the flour mixture. Add 1 tablespoon oil, 2 eggs, and 2 egg yolks. Process until the mixture forms a ball. Transfer to a floured surface.

Repeat with the remaining flour, oil, eggs, and egg yolks. Knead both batches of dough together, sprinkling with additional flour if the pasta dough is sticky. Allow the pasta dough to relax for half an hour, wrapped in plastic so it does not dry out. Use a pasta machine to roll the dough into thin sheets. Use the fettuccine roller to cut the sheets into noodles. Sprinkle with semolina flour to prevent them from sticking together.

Bring water to a boil in a 6-quart pot, add pasta, and cook until al dente. If you do not have a 6-quart pot, use a 4-quart pot and boil the pasta in 2 batches. Drain and pour into a large serving bowl. Toss with Supreme Shiitake Sauce, page 40, and serve.

Per Serving: Calories: 321, Protein: 13 gm., Fat: 8 gm., Carbohydrates: 47 gm.

Pasta with Shiitake and Rosemary

Serves 4

¼ pound fresh or reconstituted shiitake (⅔ cup), sliced, with stems removed and sliced very thin
¼ cup white wine or sparkling white grape juice
1 teaspoon olive oil
1 small garlic clove, minced
½ teaspoon rosemary, crushed
1 teaspoon low-sodium soy sauce
1 pound fresh tomatoes, chopped
½ pound fettuccine or wide egg noodles
2 tablespoons fresh parsley, minced

For pasta, bring a large pot of water to a boil. Slice mushroom stems very thin, and place in a small saucepan with white wine or grape juice and 2 tablespoons water. Cover and gently simmer until tender, 5-10 minutes.

Heat oil in a skillet over medium heat, and add sliced shiitake caps, garlic, rosemary, and soy sauce. Toss over moderate heat for 5 minutes. Add stems and tomatoes and cook over moderate heat, tossing gently until mushrooms soften, about 15 minutes. Set aside.

Cook pasta, drain, and toss with sauce.

Sprinkle with parsley.

Per Serving: Calories: 130, Protein: 4 gm., Fat: 2 gm., Carbohydrates: 23 gm.

Fettuccine with Shiitake Mushrooms

Serves 2-3

2 teaspoons olive oil

2 cloves garlic, crushed

2 tablespoons shallots, chopped

½ pound fresh or reconstituted shiitake (1⅓ cups), stems removed, sliced

¼ cup sake or dry sherry

½ cup soymilk or half-and-half

1 teaspoon low-sodium soy sauce

freshly ground black pepper to taste

½ pound fettuccine

1 tablespoon fresh parsley, minced

Heat oil in a heavy skillet, and sauté garlic and shallots for a few minutes. Add mushrooms and sauté for 15 minutes, until juice flows from mushrooms. Add the sake or sherry, soymilk, soy sauce, and pepper, and bring to a simmer for about 10 minutes.

Cook fettuccine until al dente. Drain and place in a warmed bowl.

Add sauce and sprinkle with parsley.

Per Serving: Calories: 480, Protein: 19 gm., Fat: 9 gm., Carbohydrates: 77 gm.

Pasta with Shiitake and Dried Tomatoes

Serves 4-6

½ ounce dried shiitake (½ cup)
6 sun-dried tomatoes
2 teaspoons olive oil
1 medium onion, diced
4 cloves garlic
½ teaspoon oregano
½ teaspoon rosemary
2 tablespoons fresh parsley, chopped
½ pound fresh shiitake (1⅓ cups), stems removed, chopped
freshly ground black pepper to taste
12 ounces pasta of your choice
¼ cup Parmesan cheese, grated

In a small bowl, pour enough boiling water to cover the dried shiitake and the tomatoes, and let sit for 30 minutes. Decant the mushroom soaking liquid, making sure not to pour off any grit that may remain in the bottom of the bowl, and set aside. Pat the mushrooms and tomatoes dry, and chop into large pieces.

In a large skillet, heat the oil over medium heat. When hot, add the dried mushrooms, tomatoes, onion, garlic, oregano, rosemary, and parsley. Sauté for 5 minutes. Add the fresh mushrooms and black pepper to taste. Cook on medium-high heat until the mushrooms exude their juices. Add the mushroom soaking liquid to the pan slowly, and bring to a boil. Reduce the heat and simmer for 20 minutes, stirring frequently.

In a large pot of water, boil the pasta until al dente. Drain the pasta and place in a warmed serving dish. Pour the mushroom sauce over the pasta, and garnish with Parmesan cheese.

Per Serving: Calories: 187, Protein: 7 gm., Fat: 4 gm., Carbohydrates: 31 gm.

Wild Rice Casserole with Mushrooms

Serves 6

1 cup uncooked wild rice, rinsed well

½ teaspoon leaf marjoram, crumbled

¼ teaspoon leaf thyme, crumbled

2 tablespoons olive oil

2½ cups Shiitake Stock (page 21)

1 pound fresh or reconstituted shiitake (2⅔ cups), stems removed, thinly sliced

1 medium yellow onion, peeled and chopped

1 cup plain soymilk

salt and freshly ground black pepper to taste

In a medium saucepan, sauté the rice, marjoram, and thyme in 1 tablespoon oil over moderate heat.

Pour in Shiitake Stock and bring to a boil. Adjust heat so stock simmers gently. Cover pan and cook rice for 40-45 minutes, until tender and liquid is absorbed.

Heat 1 tablespoon oil in a skillet over moderate heat. Add mushrooms and onion. Sauté, stirring frequently, for 10-12 minutes, until the juices have evaporated. Set aside.

Preheat oven to 325°F. Combine soymilk, salt, and pepper, and set mixture aside. When rice is tender, combine with the mushrooms, then with the milk mixture. Pour rice mixture into a well-greased, 2-quart casserole, cover, and bake for 30 minutes. Remove the casserole from the oven, and fluff the rice with a fork. Cover, and bake for another 30 minutes.

Per Serving: Calories: 166, Protein: 5 gm., Fat: 6 gm., Carbohydrates: 23 gm.

Shiitake Risotto

Serves 4

4 cups Shiitake Stock (page 21)

2 teaspoons olive oil

¼ cup scallions, finely minced

¼ cup onions, finely minced

1 pound fresh or reconstituted shiitake (2⅔ cups), stems
  removed, thinly sliced

1½ cups Italian Arborio rice*

salt and pepper to taste

¾ cup Parmesan cheese, freshly grated

In a heavy bottomed saucepan with a handle, over medium heat, bring the Shiitake Stock to a simmer.

In a casserole, heat the olive oil over medium heat. Add scallions and onions and sauté, stirring frequently until transparent, about 5 minutes. Add mushrooms and sauté, stirring occasionally until liquid has evaporated, about 10 minutes. Add rice to mushrooms. Add approximately ¾ cup of simmering stock to rice and mushrooms. Stir well and continue to cook, stirring frequently, until rice has absorbed most of the stock. Continue adding stock to rice ¾ cup at a time, but only after rice has absorbed previous stock. As cooking continues, stir more frequently. After 25 to 30 minutes all the stock should be absorbed, and rice should be tender but still chewy. Remove from heat.

Add salt and pepper to taste. Stir in ¼ cup of Parmesan cheese.

Serve immediately, using the rest of the cheese as a topping.

*Arborio is a generic Italian name for white rice and is shorter, thicker, and creamier than American white rice. Arborio is available in Italian groceries or food shops of many department stores.

Per Serving: Calories: 385, Protein: 15 gm., Fat: 7 gm., Carbohydrates: 63 gm.

Wild Rice Ring with Shiitake

Serves 6

1¼ cups uncooked wild rice

5 cups water

1 teaspoon salt

1 clove garlic, sliced

1 cup onions, chopped or ½ cup each onions and celery, chopped

1¼ pounds fresh shiitake (3⅓ cups), stems removed, chopped

2 tablespoons olive oil

dash nutmeg

black pepper to taste

¼ cup dry sherry

Wash wild rice well in cold water. Change several times and drain. Stir rice into 5 cups boiling water, and add salt and garlic. Reduce heat to simmer, cover, and cook without stirring until tender, about 45 minutes. Preheat oven to 350°F. Sauté onions (or onion and celery mix) and 1 cup shiitake in oil. Add a little water or vegetable broth as needed to prevent sticking. When rice is done, drain off any excess water. Add a dash of nutmeg, pepper to taste, and sherry. Mix in vegetables. Pack into a well-greased ring mold. Set mold in a pan of hot water, and bake for about 20 minutes. Loosen edge with a knife, invert onto a plate, and fill center with rest of the shiitake cut into large pieces, sautéed and seasoned as you like.

Per Serving: Calories: 229, Protein: 6 gm., Fat: 6 gm., Carbohydrates: 36 gm.

Andrew Weil

Rice with Shiitake and Pine Nuts

Serves 6

2½ cups of uncooked rice

½ cup Shiitake Stock (page 21)

1 tablespoon olive oil

2 medium onions, chopped

1 pound fresh or reconstituted shiitake (2⅔ cups), stems removed, sliced

½ cup pine nuts, lightly roasted in the oven

½ teaspoon sage

1 clove garlic, minced

salt and freshly ground black pepper to taste

Cook rice according to package directions using ½ cup Shiitake Stock in place of ½ cup water. Set cooked rice aside.

Heat oil in a heavy skillet over medium heat. Sauté onions until translucent. Add the shiitake, reduce heat to low, and cook for 15 minutes, stirring every 5 minutes or so. Add nuts, rice, sage, and garlic. Mix and season to taste with salt and pepper.

Per Serving: Calories: 385, Protein: 7 gm., Fat: 11 gm., Carbohydrates: 64 gm.

Pilaf with Shiitake Mushrooms

Serves 4

1 tablespoon extra virgin olive oil

1 cup thin vermicelli, broken into pieces

2 cups uncooked short-grain brown rice

½ medium onion, minced

1 teaspoon low-sodium soy sauce

4 cups Shiitake Stock (page 21)

¼ pound fresh or reconstituted shiitake (⅔ cup), stems removed, coarsely chopped

2 tablespoons fresh parsley, minced

In a large Dutch oven, brown noodles in olive oil. Add rice and stir well. Add onions and soy sauce. Pour boiling Shiitake Stock over rice-noodle mixture. Cook on high heat until it comes to a boil. Add fresh shiitake.

Lower heat to a simmer, and allow to steam until cooked, about 30 minutes. Fluff rice just prior to serving.

Garnish with parsley.

Per Serving: Calories: 415, Protein: 10 gm., Fat: 5 gm., Carbohydrates: 82 gm.

Green Beans, Cabbage, and Shiitake Rice

Serves 4

8 fresh or reconstituted shiitake, stems removed, coarsely chopped
1½ cups hot water
2 tablespoons peanut oil
½ teaspoon fresh ginger, minced
4 cups cabbage, coarsely chopped
1 carrot, cut in ¼-inch cubes
1 cup green beans, slivered
1 zucchini, cut in ½-inch cubes
1½ cups short-grain brown rice
¼ cup mirin or dry sherry
¼ cup low-sodium soy sauce
½ cup vegetable stock or Shiitake Stock (page 21)
3 green onions, thinly sliced

Soak the mushrooms in hot water for 30 minutes.

Strain and save 1 cup of the soaking liquid, being careful not to drain off any grit that may remain in the bottom of the pan.

Place a wok over medium-high heat. When it is hot, add the oil and ginger. Stir-fry 10 seconds. Add the mushrooms, cabbage, carrots, beans, and zucchini, and stir-fry 1 minute. Stir in the rice.

Combine the mirin or sherry, soy sauce, mushroom liquid, and vegetable stock. Pour over the rice. Bring the liquid to a boil, cover the wok, and reduce heat to low. Simmer until the rice is cooked, about 45 minutes. Transfer to a serving platter, and garnish with green onions.

Per Serving: Calories: 389, Protein: 9 gm., Fat: 7 gm., Carbohydrates: 66 gm.

❖ Main Dishes ❖

Black Bean Chili with Shiitake

Serves 8

1 pound dry black beans

3 bay leaves

1 medium onion, quartered

6 cups water

2 tablespoons olive oil

3 medium onions, chopped

2 medium green peppers, chopped

1 pound fresh or reconstituted shiitake (2⅔ cups), stems removed, chopped

6 cloves garlic, mashed

3 tablespoons cumin

3 jalapeño peppers, chopped

1 teaspoon salt

1 tablespoon paprika

2 teaspoons oregano

½ teaspoon ground cloves

3 tablespoons tomato paste

juice of one lemon

1 tablespoon honey

1 cup sour cream or soy sour cream (optional)

In a 6-quart pressure cooker, cook black beans, bay leaves, quartered onion, and water under 15 pounds pressure for 25 minutes or in an open kettle for 1½ hours. Drain liquid to ½ inch above the beans. Set aside.

Heat the oil in a large skillet, and sauté onions over medium heat for about 5 minutes. Add green peppers and shiitake. Cover and cook for 15 minutes, stirring frequently. Add garlic, cumin, jalapeño, salt, paprika, oregano, and ground cloves. Cook, stirring constantly, for 1 minute. Add this to the black beans along with the tomato paste, lemon juice, and honey. Cook on low for 30 minutes, increasing the time if you want a deeper flavor. Adjust seasoning to taste. Serve with a dollop of sour cream on top of chili, if desired.

Per Serving: Calories: 250, Protein: 10 gm., Fat: 4 gm., Carbohydrates: 42 gm.

Polenta with Shiitake Sauce

Serves 6

SHIITAKE SAUCE:

1 tablespoon olive oil

1 medium onion, chopped

¾ pound fresh or reconstituted shiitake (2 cups), stems removed, thinly sliced

1 tablespoon fresh parsley, minced

1 teaspoon fresh sage, minced

1 (12-ounce) can plum tomatoes

salt and freshly ground black pepper to taste

POLENTA:

6 cups water

2 tablespoons Shiitake Powder (page 23)

1¾ cup polenta (course cornmeal)

½ cup Parmesan cheese, grated

SAUCE:

In a saucepan, heat the oil over medium heat. Add the onion, mushrooms, parsley, and sage. Cook for 10 minutes, stirring frequently. Add the tomatoes and continue cooking for 20 minutes, until the liquid from the tomatoes evaporates. Add salt and pepper to taste. Set aside.

POLENTA:

In a saucepan, bring the water to a boil and add the Shiitake Powder. Add the polenta slowly, whisking constantly to prevent lumps. Simmer over low heat, stirring constantly, until you see the polenta begin to come away from the sides of the pan and thicken, approximately 15-20 minutes. Stir in half of the Parmesan cheese. Serve in shallow bowls, top with Shiitake Sauce, and sprinkle the remaining Parmesan cheese on top.

Per Serving: Calories: 275, Protein: 9 gm., Fat: 5 gm., Carbohydrates: 48 gm.

Steamed Shiitake Wontons

Serves 6

½ pound fresh shiitake (1⅓ cups), stems removed, cut into pieces
¼ cup green onions, minced
1 teaspoon low-sodium soy sauce
1½ teaspoons gingerroot, grated
¼ teaspoon honey
1 clove garlic, minced
24 round wonton skins (found in Asian food stores)

DIPPING SAUCE: (mix together)
2 tablespoons low-sodium soy sauce
1 teaspoon sesame oil
2 teaspoons white vinegar
1 teaspoon sugar
several drops Chinese hot pepper oil, to taste

WONTONS:

Place shiitake pieces in a food processor with green onions, soy sauce, ginger, honey, and garlic. Turn the processor on and off until finely chopped.

In the center of each wonton skin, place one teaspoon of filling. Moisten the outer edge of the wonton with water so edges will stick together. To make the wonton look like a flower, pleat the edges.

Steam the wontons over boiling water for 10 minutes.

Serve with the dipping sauce.

Per Serving: Calories: 144, Protein: 4 gm., Fat: 3 gm., Carbohydrates: 24 gm.

Broccoli, Snow Peas, and Shiitake Stir-Fry

Serves 4

6 reconstituted shiitake, stems removed

2 cups hot water

½ cup reserved mushroom soaking liquid

2 tablespoons low-sodium soy sauce

1 teaspoon mirin or dry sherry

1 teaspoon honey

1 bunch fresh broccoli

2 tablespoons peanut oil

¼ pound snow peas

1 tablespoon cornstarch

2 tablespoons cold water

Soak the shiitake in hot water for 30 minutes. Strain and reserve ½ cup of the soaking liquid for the sauce, being careful not to pour off any grit that has settled in the pan. Cut the caps in half and set aside. Mix the reserved soaking liquid, soy sauce, rice wine, and honey in a small bowl, stirring to dissolve the honey.

Rinse the broccoli and cut the tops into florets. Peel the stems and cut them diagonally in ½-inch slices.

Place a wok over medium-high heat. When it is hot, add the peanut oil. When the oil is hot, add the broccoli and mushrooms. Stir-fry 4 minutes, pour in the sauce, and bring to a boil.

Cook 2 minutes and add the snow peas. While the vegetables are cooking, dissolve the cornstarch in 2 tablespoons of cold water.

Pour into the wok and stir constantly until the sauce thickens, about 20 seconds.

Serve immediately.

Per Serving: Calories: 120, Protein: 3 gm., Fat: 7 gm., Carbohydrates: 10 gm.

Shiitake Stroganoff

Serves 4

1½ cups non-fat yogurt
1 teaspoon Dijon mustard
1½ tablespoons olive oil
2 medium onions, thinly sliced
4 cloves garlic, pressed or minced
1½ pounds fresh shiitake (4 cups), stems removed, sliced
⅓ cup dry sherry (not cooking sherry) or apple cider vinegar
salt and freshly ground black pepper to taste
paprika

In a small bowl, mix the yogurt and mustard, and set aside.

In a large sauté pan, heat the oil over medium-high heat. Add onions and cook 5 minutes until softened. Reduce heat to low and add garlic and mushrooms. Cook 10 minutes, stirring constantly. Add sherry or apple cider vinegar, and cook 10-15 minutes, until mushrooms are tender.

Remove from heat and stir in yogurt. Season with salt, pepper, and sprinkle with paprika. This is delicious over baked potatoes, rice, or noodles.

Per Serving: Calories: 238, Protein: 10 gm., Fat: 7 gm., Carbohydrates: 32 gm.

Shiitake Nut and Cheese Loaf

Makes 2 loaves (12 slices)

1 tablespoon olive oil

1 medium onion, diced

1½ pounds fresh or reconstituted shiitake (4 cups), stems removed, (or half shiitake and half button mushrooms), chopped

6 cloves garlic, chopped or pressed

1 red bell pepper, chopped

2 teaspoons thyme

1 teaspoon marjoram

½ teaspoon sage

salt and freshly ground black pepper to taste

1½ cups cooked brown rice

1½ cups walnuts, chopped (roasted in 350°F oven for 10 minutes)

½ cup cashews or sunflower seeds, chopped

4 eggs

1 cup low-fat cottage cheese

1½ pounds grated cheese: a combination of Parmesan, fontina, and/or cheddar

½ cup fresh parsley, minced

Heat oil in a large iron skillet, over medium heat and cook onion until translucent. Add mushrooms, garlic, peppers, dried herbs, salt, and pepper. Cook on medium-low heat until all the juice evaporates from the mushrooms, about 20-25 minutes.

Place mushroom mixture in a large bowl, and add rice, nuts, eggs, cottage cheese, and cheese.

Preheat oven to 350°F. Oil two 5" x 9" bread pans. Pack the mixture into the pans. Bake 1 hour, until firm. Remove from oven and let cool on rack for 10 minutes. Remove the loaves from the pans. Garnish with fresh parsley.

Great with ketchup or Supreme Shiitake Sauce, page 40—tastes like Mom's old-fashioned meat loaf!

Per Slice: Calories: 387, Protein: 27 gm., Fat: 23 gm., Carbohydrates: 17 gm.

Stir-Fried Dried Shiitake

Serves 4 as a side dish

12 dried shiitake

SAUCE
2 tablespoons tamari
1 tablespoon sake
2 teaspoons honey
½ pound snow peas
1 teaspoon canola oil
1 cup bamboo shoots, sliced

Soak shiitake in enough boiling water to cover for 15 minutes. Save liquid for flavoring soups, being careful not to pour off any grit that may remain in the pan. Leave small mushrooms whole and cut large ones in half.

Mix tamari, sake, and honey; set aside.

In a wok, stir-fry snow pea pods in oil over high heat, until bright green but still crunchy. Remove pea pods and set aside.

Heat the wok with the remaining oil from the pea pods, and stir-fry mushrooms and bamboo shoots over medium-high heat for 5 minutes. Add sauce, pea pods, and mix well.

Per Serving: Calories: 81, Protein: 4 gm., Fat: 1 gm., Carbohydrates: 14 gm.

Mushroom Cheese Crêpes with Bechamel Sauce

Makes 16 to 18 crêpes

CRÊPES
3 eggs
1 cup skim milk
1 tablespoon canola oil
¾ cup unbleached flour

BECHAMEL SAUCE
1 tablespoon butter
1 tablespoon flour
2½ cups skim milk
pinch of salt
⅛ teaspoon ground red pepper
1½ cups low-fat Monterey Jack cheese, shredded
freshly grated nutmeg, to taste

To make the crêpes in advance:

In a medium bowl, combine eggs, milk, oil, and flour until smooth. Refrigerate mixture 30 minutes. The batter should be the consistency of heavy cream. If it isn't, thin with additional milk.

Heat a 6- or 7-inch crêpe pan or other flat-bottomed frying pan over medium heat. Wipe the bottom of the pan with a paper towel dipped in canola oil to coat the surface of the pan. When the pan is hot enough to make a few drops of water sizzle, pour in about 2 tablespoons of the batter, tilting the pan so batter flows quickly over the entire surface. Cook until the top surface of crêpe looks dry and edge is slightly browned. Flip and cook the underside briefly. Repeat with remaining batter. Stack crêpes on a plate as they are completed, layering with wax paper.

To prepare bechamel sauce:

Melt butter in a large saucepan over medium-low heat. Stir in flour and cook for about 1 minute, stirring. Remove from heat and slowly add milk, whisking until blended. Season with salt and red pepper. Cook, stirring, until sauce bubbles and thickens, stirring frequently. Set aside.

FILLING:
1 tablespoon canola oil
1 pound fresh shiitake (2⅔ cups), stems removed, thinly sliced
2 shallots or green onions, thinly sliced
1 small clove garlic, minced
1 teaspoon fresh basil, minced
½ cup dry sherry
salt and freshly ground black pepper to taste
lemon juice to taste

To make the filling:

In a wide frying pan, heat oil over medium-high heat. Add mushrooms, shallot, and garlic. Cook, stirring often, until mushrooms are lightly browned and liquid evaporates, about 15 minutes. Lift out ¼ cup mushrooms and set aside for garnish.

Add basil, stir in sherry, and cook until the liquid is reduced to a syrup sauce. Remove from heat and season to taste with salt, pepper, and lemon juice.

Spoon an equal amount of filling down the center of each crêpe, and fold over the sides. Place a single layer of crêpes, seam side down, in a lightly greased 9" x 13" baking pan. Preheat oven to 400°F.

Add cheese and nutmeg to bechamel sauce. Cook, stirring often, over medium heat until sauce is heated through. Brush sauce over crêpes saving about 1 cup for serving.

Bake, uncovered, for 12 to 15 minutes or until lightly browned and bubbly. Spoon some sauce onto each plate, and serve the crêpes with the reserved mushrooms on top.

Per Serving: Calories: 164, Protein: 9 gm., Fat: 8 gm., Carbohydrates: 11 gm.

Baked Tomatoes Stuffed with Mushrooms

Serves 2-3

6 ripe medium tomatoes

¼ teaspoon salt

¼ teaspoon freshly ground black pepper

1 pound fresh or reconstituted shiitake (2⅔ cups), stems removed, finely minced

⅓ cup onion, minced

2 tablespoons olive oil

2 tablespoons flour

1 tablespoon Madeira or sherry

¼ cup yogurt

1 teaspoon low-sodium soy sauce

pepper

2 tablespoons Parmesan cheese, freshly grated

Using a sharp knife, slice tops off tomatoes and hollow out, leaving shells about ⅜-inch thick. Save tomato pulp to use for stuffing. Combine ¼ teaspoon salt and ¼ teaspoon pepper. Rub the inside of each tomato shell with the mixture.

Set the tomatoes upside-down to drain.

Prepare the stuffing:

Strain the tomato pulp and mince. Sauté shiitake, onion, and minced tomato in oil in a medium skillet over moderate heat for 25 to 30 minutes, stirring frequently, until most of the juices have reduced. When the mixture is fairly dry, stir in flour, Madeira, yogurt, soy sauce, and pepper to taste. Cook, stirring constantly, over low heat for about 5 minutes. Preheat the oven to 350°F. Stuff each tomato with the mushroom mixture, spooning it in lightly and mounding it up slightly on top. Sprinkle each stuffed tomato with grated Parmesan cheese. Stand the tomatoes in an ungreased, 9-inch pie plate, and bake them, uncovered, for 30 minutes or until the cheese is lightly browned.

Per Serving: Calories: 330, Protein: 11 gm., Fat: 12 gm., Carbohydrates: 40 gm.

Shiitake Kebobs

Serves 4-6

1 pound medium-sized fresh shiitake (2 ⅔ cups), stems removed

1 pineapple, cut into ½-inch cubes

2 peppers, green and red, cut into squares

¼ pound cherry tomatoes

½ pound new potatoes, pre-cooked in boiling water for 10
   minutes, and quartered

wooden skewers, soaked in water

MARINADE

½ cup olive oil

3 tablespoons red wine vinegar

1 clove garlic, minced

1 teaspoon mustard

salt and freshly ground black pepper to taste

1 tablespoon fresh parsley

1 tablespoon marjoram, finely chopped

Prepare the marinade by adding all the ingredients together, and set aside.

Cut the stems off the shiitake, and set aside. Small shiitake are the easiest to use; if you only find large ones, cut them into quarters.

Toss vegetables in the marinade once before placing on the skewers. Thread the vegetables onto the skewers alternating with shiitake.

Place kebobs on a medium-hot grill. Baste every 2 minutes with marinade while cooking, and turn until lightly browned.

These will be ready in about 5-10 minutes, depending on the heat of the fire.

Try other vegetables such as zucchini, eggplant, fresh asparagus, and onions.

Per Serving: Calories: 266, Protein: 4 gm., Fat: 11 gm., Carbohydrates: 36 gm.

Shiitake Tempura

Serves 4

TEMPURA BATTER
½ cup flour
½ cup cornstarch
pinch of salt
1½ teaspoons baking powder
2 egg whites
1 cup water, plus one ice cube

½ pound fresh shiitake (1⅓ cups), stems removed
canola oil
1 daikon, grated*
Shiitake Tempura Dipping Sauce (page 45)

TEMPURA BATTER:

Mix dry ingredients. Beat egg whites with water, and add to dry mix. Do not over-mix. Batter should be very thin. (Prepare just before frying.)

Dip fresh shiitake in batter, one by one, drain excess batter, and fry quickly in hot oil until golden. The temperature of the oil should be between 350°F and 375°F and deep enough to cover the shiitake. If the oil smokes, it is too hot. Drain on paper towels.

Serve with grated daikon and Shiitake Tempura Dipping Sauce on the side.

Since this recipe makes a generous amount of batter it is recommended to prepare a few other vegetables, such as yam slices, onion rings, asparagus spears, or zucchini slices.

*white Japanese radish

Per Serving: Calories: 261, Protein: 3 gm., Fat: 13 gm., Carbohydrates: 30 gm.

Shiitake Potato Pancakes

Serves 8

*For a supremely excellent shiitake flavor
serve this as soon as possible after frying.*

3 medium-sized potatoes, peeled

2 pounds fresh or reconstituted shiitake (5⅓ cups), sliced in thin
    strips

1 small onion, minced

4 eggs, slightly beaten

2 tablespoons low-fat milk

3-4 tablespoons flour

salt and freshly ground black pepper to taste

4 teaspoons extra virgin olive oil

1 cup apple sauce

Grate raw potatoes and rinse under water. Squeeze to drain the excess
moisture. Place the potatoes in a large bowl, and add all the ingredients
except the oil and apple sauce.

In a large, non-stick skillet, heat 1 teaspoon oil on medium-high, and measure
out enough mix to make 4-inch pancakes. Press down the center of the
patties, so they will cook evenly. Fry until golden brown. Add additional oil,
1 teaspoon at a time, as needed.

Serve immediately with a spoonful of apple sauce on the side.

Per Serving: Calories: 191, Protein: 8 gm., Fat: 4 gm., Carbohydrates: 25 gm.

Rice Salad with Many Mushrooms

Serves 8 to 10

½ cup uncooked wild rice
2 cups water
2 cups uncooked brown or white rice
4 cups water
½ cup fresh oyster mushrooms
½ cup fresh or reconstituted shiitake, stems removed
½ cup fresh enoki "straw" mushrooms
¼ cup wood ears, dried
1 tablespoon olive oil
1 clove garlic, minced
½ bunch scallions, thinly sliced
½ cup pine nuts, toasted
freshly ground black pepper and salt to taste

VINAIGRETTE
3 tablespoons olive oil
1 tablespoon sesame oil
2 tablespoons soy sauce
3 tablespoons fresh gingerroot, grated
3 cloves garlic, minced
juice of 1 lemon
¼ cup rice vinegar

Cook wild and white rice separately following standard recipes. For brown rice and wild rice: Rinse the rice very well. Combine rice and water in a heavy-bottomed, 2-quart pot with a tight fitting lid. Bring to a boil. Cover, turn the heat down to a simmer, and cook for 45 minutes until all water is absorbed. Cooking time for white rice is much shorter. Set aside. Remove tough stems from shiitake. Wood ears and shiitake take about 20 minutes to reconstitute in boiling water. In a sauté pan, cook the oyster and shiitake mushrooms in 1 tablespoon olive oil and garlic for about 10 minutes. Add the enoki and wood ears for the last 2 minutes of the sauté.

Prepare the vinaigrette in a medium bowl by whisking together the olive oil, sesame oil, soy sauce, grated gingerroot, garlic, lemon juice, and vinegar. While the rice is still warm, add the vinaigrette until rice is well-coated but not soggy. Mix in the scallions, pine nuts, and all mushrooms except enoki. Add salt and pepper to taste. The straw mushrooms are fragile and should be placed on top of the salad as a garnish. If you have some fresh enoki, a small clump can be placed on top.

Per Serving: Calories: 296, Protein: 5 gm., Fat: 12 gm., Carbohydrates: 39 gm.

Whole Wheat Pizza Dough

Makes dough for two 12-inch pizzas

1 package dry yeast
¾ cup lukewarm water
1 cup white flour
¾ cup whole wheat flour
pinch of salt
2 tablespoons olive oil

Dissolve yeast in ¼ cup lukewarm water. In a large bowl, combine white flour, whole wheat flour, and salt. Stir in ½ cup warm water, oil, and the yeast mixture. Mix until it forms a moist dough, then knead on a floured surface for 10 minutes until it is smooth. Put dough in an oiled bowl, turning to coat the surface of the ball. Let it rise, covered, in a warm place for one hour or until doubled in bulk. Punch dough down and press out in very lightly oiled pizza pans

You can wrap half the dough in plastic and freeze until ready to use. Defrost 4-6 hours until room temperature.

Per ¼ pizza crust : Calories: 117, Protein: 3 gm., Fat: 3 gm., Carbohydrates: 18 gm.

Jo Riley

Deep Dish Shiitake Pizza

Makes 1 pizza

½ pound fresh shiitake (1⅓ cups), stems removed

1 tablespoon olive oil

2 cloves garlic, chopped

3 tablespoons fresh parsley, minced

½ recipe Whole Wheat Pizza Dough (page 94)

½ cup mozzarella, grated

¼ cup dried tomatoes, rehydrated in warm water and chopped

¼ cup Parmesan cheese, grated

Sauté shiitake in oil over medium heat until tender. After 10 minutes, add garlic and parsley. Set aside.

Prepare Whole Wheat Pizza Dough, roll out, and line the bottom and sides of a 12-inch, deep-dish pizza pan. Brush it with olive oil, and sprinkle on grated mozzarella. Spread the dried tomatoes over the cheese. Add the mushroom mixture and top with freshly grated Parmesan cheese.

Preheat oven to 425°F. Bake for 15-20 minutes or until the bottom is crisp and browned.

Per Serving: Calories: 282, Protein: 11 gm., Fat: 11 gm., Carbohydrates: 33 gm.

Deep Fried Stuffed Shiitake

Serves 8

½ pound tofu
20 fresh shiitake, stems removed
flour to dust the shiitake
1 carrot, minced
1 green onion, minced
1 egg, lightly beaten
1 teaspoon flour
½ teaspoon arrowroot
1 teaspoon sesame oil
black pepper to taste
canola oil for deep-frying

Dice tofu into ¼-inch cubes, parboil, and pat dry. Set aside.

Choose the largest 15 shiitake to stuff, and set aside. Mince the remaining 5 shiitake. Dust insides of mushrooms with flour.

In a medium bowl, combine the tofu with the minced shiitake, carrots, and green onion. Add the egg, flour, arrowroot, sesame oil and pepper to taste, and mix well. In a deep skillet or wok, heat the oil to 350°F, and deep-fry the shiitake. Turn the shiitake caps gill side up, and fill with the tofu mixture about 1 inch high, patting down the top and sides to firm. Return the stuffed shiitake to the oil, gill side up and deep-fry for thirty seconds. Take the shiitake out of the oil, and place on paper toweling to drain. Serve immediately.

Per Serving: Calories: 118, Protein: 4 gm., Fat: 8 gm., Carbohydrates: 6 gm.

Ragout of Mushrooms

Serves 6

2 teaspoons olive oil

1 large onion, chopped

2 carrots, chopped

2 celery stalks, chopped

4 cloves garlic, minced

1 cup red wine

salt and freshly ground black pepper to taste

½ pound fresh or reconstituted shiitake (1⅓ cups), stems removed

1 pound button mushrooms

3 tablespoons flour

3 cups Shiitake Stock (page 21)

2 tablespoons half-and-half

2 tablespoons fresh parsley, chopped

several sprigs fresh rosemary

In a heavy saucepan, sauté 1 teaspoon oil and the onion, over medium heat, until the onion is translucent, about 10 minutes. Add the garlic, carrots and celery. Cook another 15 minutes on medium heat, stirring frequently. Add the wine and salt and pepper to taste. Cook to reduce the liquid by half.

Heat 1 teaspoon oil in a large skillet, and add the mushrooms. Stir frequently and keep the lid on the skillet; this will help the mushrooms exude their juices quickly. Cook the mushrooms until they are soft, about 15 minutes. Add the mushrooms to the vegetable mixture, and add the flour. Cook for a few minutes.

Add the Shiitake Stock. Cook over medium heat for 30 minutes. Remove from the heat and add the half-and-half.

Sprinkle with parsley and rosemary and serve.

Per Serving: Calories: 115, Protein: 3 gm., Fat: 2 gm., Carbohydrates: 15 gm.

Chop Suey

Serves 4

2 tablespoons peanut oil

¼ pound fresh or reconstituted shiitake (⅔ cup), stems removed, sliced

a total of 1½ pounds of any combination of the following vegetables:

cabbage bok choy, chopped

bean sprouts

bamboo shoots

water chestnuts, sliced

watercress

celery, sliced

carrot strips

broccoli florets

green onions, chopped

garlic cloves, sliced

green peppers, cubed

2 tablespoons corstarch and water (½ cup)

2 cubes vegetable bouillon

2 tablespoons low-sodium soy sauce

1 teaspoons sugar

black pepper to taste

In a wok or large frying pan, heat the oil until very hot, but not smoking. Add the vegetables and quickly stir-fry at high temperature for 3-5 minutes.

Stir water into corstarch, then gradually stir in vegetable bouillon, soy sauce, and sugar. Add bouillon mixture to the vegetables, and toss. Add pepper to taste.

Per Serving: Calories: 157, Protein: 4 gm., Fat: 7 gm., Carbohydrates: 19 gm.

Tofu and Shiitake Patties

Makes 12 patties

1 pound firm tofu
6 shiitake, stems removed, cut into thin strips
1 carrot, cut into matchsticks
1 tablespoon arrowroot powder or cornstarch
salt and freshly ground black pepper

In a large bowl, crumble the tofu and add the shiitake, carrots, and arrowroot. Season with salt and pepper. Form the tofu mixture into patties, 2 inches across.

Place under the broiler in the oven for a few minutes until lightly browned; turn over to brown the other side.

Serve hot with soy sauce or ketchup.

Per Serving: Calories: 40, Protein: 3 gm., Fat: 1 gm., Carbohydrates: 3 gm.

Gorgonzola-Onion Shiitake Pizza

Serves 4

½ recipe Whole Wheat Pizza Dough (page 94), or pre-baked pizza
    crust
1 teaspoon olive oil
1 medium onion, sliced
¼ pound fresh shiitake (⅔ cup), stems removed, thinly sliced
12-15 dried tomato halves
¼ cup water
¾ pound gorgonzola cheese, grated
rosemary leaves, crushed
1 teaspoon fresh rosemary, finely chopped

Prepare pizza dough and set aside.

In a sauté pan, sauté ½ teaspoon olive oil and the onion over medium heat, and gently cook for ½ hour, until brown and caramelized. Set aside.

In another sauté pan, sauté ½ teaspoon olive oil and shiitake 15 minutes over medium-low heat or until tender. Set aside.

Make a puree of the dried tomatoes and water in a blender. Add water as needed to make it smooth. Spread a thin layer of tomato puree over the pizza dough surface. Cover with a layer of caramelized onions. Add the shiitake and top with gorgonzola cheese.

Sprinkle with rosemary.

Preheat oven to 450°F and bake 8 to 10 minutes or until the bottom is crisp and browned.

Per Serving: Calories: 484, Protein: 25 gm., Fat: 21 gm., Carbohydrates: 42 gm.

❖ Side Dishes ❖

Avocados Stuffed with Goat Cheese and Shiitake

Serves 8

6 ounces soft goat cheese (chèvre)
2 tablespoons sun-dried tomatoes, chopped
1 tablespoon fresh basil, chopped
4 small ripe avocados
1 teaspoon olive oil
½ pound fresh shiitake (1⅓ cups), stems removed, coarsely
    chopped

In a small bowl, mix goat cheese, sun-dried tomatoes, and basil; set aside.

Halve and pit avocados. Scoop out some of the avocado, leaving a ½-inch thick shell. Set avocado shells aside. Coarsely chop avocado and add to cheese mixture.

In a small frying pan, sauté oil and mushrooms for 5 minutes.

Preheat oven to 400°F. Reserve a few mushrooms for garnish, then divide the rest equally among the avocado shells.

Top with cheese mixture, spreading it evenly to fill shells. Top with reserved mushrooms.

Bake 15 minutes or until filling is hot.

Per Serving: Calories: 249, Protein: 6 gm., Fat: 18 gm., Carbohydrates: 13 gm.

Sautéed Shiitake

Serves 4

1 pound fresh or reconstituted shiitake, stems removed, whole,
   sliced, or grated, as you prefer
1 tablespoon light olive oil

In a large, cast iron sauté pan, warm the oil over a medium-low heat. Higher temperatures cause the shiitake to become tough. Add the shiitake, and toss to coat with the oil. Stir every few minutes or shake pan and continue cooking and stirring until the shiitake liquid evaporates.

There are two ways to know when the shiitake are ready. First, there will be an iridescent quality to the liquid surrounding the mushrooms; second, the texture of the mushroom will be very tender. This takes approximately 10-15 minutes.

Per Serving: Calories: 96, Protein: 3 gm., Fat: 3 gm., Carbohydrates: 12 gm.

Barbecued Shiitake–Japanese Style

12 fresh shiitake

SHIITAKE DIPPING SAUCE
Combine:
3 tablespoons low-sodium soy sauce
3 tablespoons sake or dry sherry
3 tablespoons water
ginger to taste
garlic to taste

Barbecue the shiitake on a medium-hot grill, with the gills turned up. Keep stems on; they make góod handles for serving.

The shiitake are ready when the gills have beads of water on them, about 5-8 minutes. Remove the shiitake to plates, and dip into the sauce.

Per Serving: Calories: 22, Protein: 1 gm., Fat: 0 gm., Carbohydrates: 3 gm.

Creamed Shiitake

Serves 4

Prepare the white sauce before sautéing the mushrooms. If you wish a richer dish, add the optional egg to the white sauce.

WHITE SAUCE
1 cup milk
1 bay leaf
4 peppercorns
1 large piece of lemon peel
1 tablespoon butter
1 tablespoon flour
1 egg, beaten (optional)
Salt and freshly ground white pepper to taste

1 tablespoon light olive oil
½ pound fresh or reconstituted shiitake (1⅓ cups), sliced
1 cup white sauce
1 tablespoon fresh parsley, coarsely chopped

Combine the milk, bay leaf, peppercorns, and lemon peel in a saucepan, and slowly bring to a boil. Lower heat and simmer slowly for 15 minutes. Take off the heat, cover, and let sit. Melt the butter, stir in the flour, and cook over medium heat for a minute, stirring. Strain spices out of warm milk and gradually whisk into flour along with beaten egg, if used. Season with salt and pepper. Place sauce in a double-boiler, and simmer for 15 minutes.

In a sauté pan, heat oil over medium-low heat. Sauté mushrooms 10-15 minutes until they are tender and exude their juices. Pour the white sauce over the mushrooms. Remove from heat, mix well, place on a serving dish, and top with chopped parsley.

Per Serving: Calories: 121, Protein: 4 gm., Fat: 8 gm., Carbohydrates: 10 gm.

Mushrooms with Duxelles Stuffing

WHITE SAUCE

1 tablespoon butter

1 tablespoon flour

½ cup half-and-half

⅔ cup milk

3 tablespoons fresh parsley, finely chopped

1 tablespoon fresh basil, chopped

¾ pound fresh or reconstituted shiitake mushrooms (2 cups), stems removed finely chopped

4 tablespoons shallots or scallions, finely chopped

1 tablespoon olive oil

1 teaspoon fresh parsley, finely chopped

salt and freshly ground black pepper to taste

18 to 24 two-inch fresh button mushroom caps

2 tablespoons dry bread crumbs, finely crumbled

1 tablespoon Swiss cheese, grated

WHITE SAUCE:

In a small saucepan, melt the butter, stir in the flour, and cook over medium heat for a minute, stirring. Slowly add the half-and-half, milk, and herbs. Cook over low heat until slightly thickened. Set aside.

Squeeze the chopped shiitake, a handful at a time, in the corner of a towel to extract as much liquid as possible. Set aside.

In a heavy, 8"-10" skillet, cook the shallots in oil over moderate heat, stirring constantly, for 2 minutes or until they are soft. Add the chopped mushrooms and cook, stirring occasionally, for 15-20 minutes or until all the moisture has evaporated and the mushrooms are beginning to brown lightly. With a rubber spatula, transfer the mixture to a large bowl; stir in the White Sauce, parsley, and salt and pepper to taste. Preheat oven to 350°F. Oil a large, shallow baking dish or roasting pan. Fill mushroom caps with shiitake mixture. Mix the bread crumbs and grated cheese, then sprinkle them over the filling. Arrange the caps in the pan. Bake in the upper third of the oven for 10 to 15 minutes or until the mushrooms are tender and the filling is lightly browned. Serve hot or cold.

Per Serving: Calories: 45, Protein: 2 gm., Fat: 2 gm., Carbohydrates: 4 gm.

Chinese Creamed Cabbage and Shiitake

Serves 4

1 tablespoon butter

1 tablespoon flour

1 cup half-and-half

1 tablespoon oil

whole garlic clove and a slice of gingerroot, pierced with toothpick for easy removal

1 pound Chinese cabbage (napa), sliced lengthwise

salt and freshly ground black pepper to taste

6 fresh or reconstituted shiitake, stems removed

several parboiled peas or cherry tomatoes for garnish

In a small saucepan, melt the butter and blend in the flour for the white sauce. Slowly add the half-and-half. Cook until slightly thickened. Set aside.

In a large skillet, heat the oil, and add garlic and gingerroot. Add and sauté cabbage, salt, and pepper for about 3-5 minutes. Add shiitake and sauté 1 minute more. Discard garlic and gingerroot. Remove cabbage to a warm serving platter, and top with warm white sauce.

Place shiitake attractively on sauce. Decorate with peas or cherry tomatoes.

Per Serving: Calories: 189, Protein: 4 gm., Fat: 13 gm., Carbohydrates: 14 gm.

Greens and Shiitake

Serves 4

1 pound spinach or other greens
1 tablespoon oil
2 tablespoons low-sodium soy sauce
freshly ground black pepper to taste
¼ pound shiitake (⅔ cup), thickly sliced

Thoroughly clean the spinach, cut into 3-inch pieces, and set aside.

In a large skillet, sauté spinach, soy sauce, and pepper in oil over a medium-high heat for 3 minutes. Add the shiitake and cook for 5 minutes. Shiitake should be a little chewy and the greens just cooked.

Per Serving: Calories: 68, Protein: 3 gm., Fat: 3 gm., Carbohydrates: 6 gm.

Barbecued Shiitake

Serves 4

½ pound fresh shiitake (1⅓ cups), stems left on

Grill fresh shiitake over red-hot charcoal 2 to 3 inches above coals, gill side up. Cook until gills sweat beads of moisture and caps begin to darken. Turn over. Brush caps with barbecue sauce (suggestions follow), and continue cooking until gill side begins to brown. Turn over again and brush a little more sauce on gills. Mushrooms should be cooked but still chewy, not crisp. Keep stems on; they make good handles for serving.

SAUCE IDEAS:

1) Szechuan style: mix dark sesame oil, soy sauce, ginger, garlic, chili paste, or ground red chili powder, honey to taste, wine vinegar.

2) For those who don't like it hot, omit chili and add dry sherry or sake.

3) Use your favorite tomato-based barbecue sauce.

Per Serving: Calories: 33, Protein: 1 gm., Fat: 0 gm., Carbohydrates: 6 gm.

Andrew Weil

Shiitake Cooked in Aluminum Foil

Serves 2 to 4

8 to 10 fresh shiitake, sliced ¼-inch thick

DIPPING SAUCE
Combine:
3 tablespoons low-sodium soy sauce
2 tablespoons light sesame oil
½ teaspoon sugar
1 teaspoon roasted and crushed sesame seeds

Place the mushrooms in the center of a 12" x 24" inch piece of aluminium foil. Wrap the mushrooms, creating a neat package with the ends folded over to capture the steam.

Cook 4 inches over a medium-hot grill or a gas burner on low, until steam begins to come out the top of the package. The mushrooms are cooked in about 8-10 minutes.

Serve immediately with the dipping sauce.

Per Serving: Calories: 143, Protein: 4 gm., Fat: 9 gm., Carbohydrates: 11 gm.

Broiled Shiitake

Serves 4

Shiitake essence at its best.

½ pound fresh shiitake (1⅓ cups), stems removed
Salt

Preheat broiler. Select choice quality fresh shiitake.

Place shiitake on a baking sheet gill side up. Salt very lightly. Broil until there are beads of moisture on the gills. Watch closely; this takes a few minutes. Serve immediately before shiitake become dried out.

Per Serving: Calories: 33, Protein: 1 gm., Fat: 0 gm., Carbohydrates: 6 gm.

Baked Shiitake and Cheese

Serves 4 to 6

8 fresh shiitake, stems removed, thickly sliced
½ teaspoon oil
½ cup dry white wine
6 tablespoons fresh parsley, minced
2 cloves garlic, minced
½ teaspoon dried basil
⅔ cup Jarlsberg or Swiss cheese, shredded
fresh parsley, minced, for garnish

Preheat oven to 400°F. Spread ½ teaspoon oil on the bottom of a large, shallow baking dish. Arrange mushrooms in a single layer in dish.

In a small saucepan, heat wine, parsley, garlic, and basil. Pour over mushrooms. Bake, covered, 25-30 minutes or until mushrooms are very tender. Sprinkle with cheese and bake 2-3 minutes longer. Serve hot, sprinkled with additional parsley.

Per Serving: Calories: 128, Protein: 8 gm., Fat: 6 gm., Carbohydrates: 5 gm.

Herbs with Shiitake

Serves 4

1 teaspoons oil
½ pound fresh shiitake (1⅓ cups), stems removed, sliced
½ teaspoon low-sodium soy sauce
½ teaspoon herbs (a mixture of basil, rosemary, sage, and thyme)
dash of dry mustard powder
1 tablespoon red wine vinegar

In a medium skillet, sauté oil, sliced mushrooms, soy sauce, herbs, and mustard for 15 minutes on medium-low heat. Add vinegar and cook for 5 minutes.

Per Serving: Calories: 44, Protein: 1 gm., Fat: 2 gm., Carbohydrates: 7 gm.

Sweet Shiitake

Serves 4 to 6

10 large shiitake, reconstituted, stems removed
½ tablespoon sugar
2 teaspoons low-sodium soy sauce
1 tablespoon mirin

After soaking the shiitake, cut the stems completely off the mushroom. If the caps are large, cut into pie-shaped wedges. Pour the mushroom soaking liquid into a saucepan, and boil. Add the shiitake and sugar, and stir for 5 minutes. Add soy sauce and simmer another 5 minutes. Add the mirin before removing from the heat. Place the shiitake and liquid in a dish, and let sit for 10-15 minutes to soak up the flavors before serving.

Per Serving: Calories: 32, Protein: 1 gm., Fat: 0 gm., Carbohydrates: 6 gm.

Creamed Shiitake on Toast

Serves 4

1 large shallot, minced
1 teaspoon oil
¼ pound fresh shiitake (⅔ cup), sliced
2 tablespoons vermouth (optional)
1 egg yolk (optional)
½ cup half-and-half
lemon juice
pinch of crushed, dried red peppers
2 tablespoons fresh parsley, chopped
2 teaspoons marjoram
4 slices hot toast

Sauté the shallot in 1 teaspoon of oil until soft. Add the mushrooms, raise the heat slightly, and cook for 1 minute, tossing to coat the mushrooms. Add the vermouth, if desired, and cook for 1 minute longer. Reduce the heat to low.

In a small bowl, combine the egg yolk and half-and-half, and add to the mushrooms. Add the lemon juice and peppers, and cook over very low heat until the mixture thickens. Do not let it boil.

Garnish with parsley and marjoram. Serve the mushrooms over the toast.

Per Serving: Calories: 136, Protein: 5 gm., Fat: 6 gm., Carbohydrates: 16 gm.

Appendix 1

Nutritional Value of Mushrooms

Shiitake, as with all mushrooms, are extremely high in water content. This means that while the composition of shiitake may be very nutritious, the fact that they contain between 85% and 90% moisture means that a considerable amount have to be eaten to obtain enough nutrients to serve as a main staple in one's diet. The quality of the food value is high however. An article in *Shiitake News* summarized the literature on the subject of shiitake nutrition by combining a literature search on the subject with data accumulated from analysis of shiitake grown outdoors in Wisconsin.[5] In addition to water, shiitake are about 14% carbohydrate, 2.14% protein and .46% fat. On a dry weight basis this computes to 76% carbohydrate, 16% protein, 2.45% fat and 7.06% moisture.

Protein
Since protein is measured as a function of nitrogen content and mushrooms contain a large amount of chitin which also contains nitrogen, the true protein is only about 70% of the apparent protein content. This means the digestible protein is therefore 1.5% of the fresh mushroom and about 11.2% of the dried product.

Fatty Acid
The main fat in shiitake is linoleic acid (75%) with minor amounts of palmitic, stearic, and oleic acids. Linoleic is the only essential fatty acid for human food consumption.

Vitamins

Water-Soluble
Relatively small amounts of water-soluble vitamins, such as ascorbic acid, riboflavin, and thiamin, are found in shiitake, though they are present—see Table III. Niacin is the only water soluble vitamin found in any quantity. Studies in Wisconsin showed a higher content than previously reported in the literature—6.2mg in fresh and 27.8 mg in dried per 100 gms of mushroom. This translates to a 30% of the recommended daily allowance.

Fat-Soluble

The fat-soluble vitamins are present in very small amounts, with the exception of ergosterol, which is converted to vitamin D in the presence of ultra violet light. The ergosterol content measured 52.28 mg/gm of fresh mushrooms and 452 mg/gm of dried shiitake in the Wisconsin grown mushrooms. What is most significant is that the fat content of shiitake, while higher than most other mushrooms, is still very low in saturated fats.

Vitamins	Fresh (mg/100g)	Freeze Dried (mg/100g)
Ascorbic Acid	2.72	3.45
Riboflavin	0.19	1.67
Thiamin	0.08	0.53
Niacin	6.20	27.83
a-tocopherol	<.01	<.01
b-carotene	<.01	<.01

Minerals

Eight minerals were measured in the Wisconsin research: sodium, copper, magnesium, iron, calcium, potassium, manganese, and zinc. The results of this work indicated a slightly higher amount of minerals than earlier reports. Shiitake tends to be rather low in iron and high in calcium which agrees with the data from the dried material. Magnesium and potassium are present in substantial enough quantities to consider these materials as sufficient to supplement dietary need—22% for magnesium and 50-100% for potassium.

Minerals	Fresh (mg/100g)	Freeze Dried (mg/100g)
Na	30.05	26.31
Cu	1.19	0.53
Mg	86.42	151.25
Fe	1.86	1.16
Ca	1.79	14.87
K	2180.43	2397.25
Mn	2.25	1.49
Zn	5.47	4.41

Amino Acids

Shiitake mushrooms contain all of the essential amino acids making them a complete protein. However, they are low in the sulfur-containing amino acids, so they are not adequate as your sole source of protein. When eaten together, legumes and shiitake balance out each others amino acid deficiencies.

Amino Acid	Free Amino Acid (mg/g)	Total Amino Acid (mg/g)
Lysine	1.00	3.41
Phenylalanine	0.68	2.88
Leucine	1.27	5.06
Isoleucine	0.78	3.38
Methionine	0.14	0.90
Valine	0.95	3.83
Threonine	0.34	5.20
Arginine	1.23	5.20
Histidine	0.48	1.82
Tyrosine	0.41	1.06
Proline	0.94	3.57
Alanine	0.90	4.10
Glycine	0.80	4.01
Serine	0.06	1.38
Glutamic acid	3.90	14.17
Aspartic acid	1.87	8.33

Carbohydrates

While a high percentage of the non-water content of shiitake is carbohydrate and fiber (76% dry weight basis), the majority of this is indigestible. Of the carbohydrates, fiber constitutes about 13%[6].The majority of the fiber is in the form of chitin, which is not digestible by humans and serves as a laxative in the diet. Shiitake contains a significant amount of the dietary type of fiber necessary for good health. Most interesting is the fact that Donko shiitake contain about 25% more of this type of fiber than the other grades. Carbohydrates are found in both the 5 carbon configuration (xylose and ribose) and in the 6 carbon form (glucose, galactose, and mannose), as well as some 10 carbon forms.

The following information is from *The Biology and Cultivation of Edible Mushrooms*, S.T. Chang, WA Hayes Academic Press, NY 1978 Chapter 6 Nutritional Value. Eli V Crisan and Anne Sands PP 137-168

Table I Proximate Composition of Cultivated and Wild Species of Edible Mushrooms presented as % of dry weight except initial moisture and energy values

Species	Sample	Initial Moisture	Crude Protein	Fat	Carbohydrate Total	N-Free	Fiber	Ash	Energy Value kcal
L. edodes	Fresh[1]	90.0	17.5	8	67.5	59.5	8	7	387
	Fresh[2]	91.8	13.4	4.9	78.0	70.7	7.3	3.7	392
	*nd[3]	*nd	13.3	4.8	78.5	71.4	7.1	3.4	393
	Dried[4]	18.4	13.1	1.2	79.2	64.5	14.7	6.5	333
	Dried[5]	15.8	10.3	1.9	82.3	75.8	6.5	5.5	375

*nd = not determined

1. Sawada. (1965) Todai Enshurin Hokoku 59, 33 and Sugimori, T., Oyama, Y., and Omichi, T. (1971). Studies on basidiomycetes. 1. Productions of mycelium and fruiting body from noncarbohydrate organic substances. J. Ferment. Technol. 49, 435-446

2. Food and Agricultural Organization (1972). "Food Composition Table for Use in East Asia." Food Policy and Nutr. Div., Food Agric. Organ. U.N., Rome

3. Singer, R. and Harris, B., *Mushrooms and Truffles*, Koeltz Scientific Books, Königstein Germany, 1987, p 173 and Sawada (1965). Todai Enshurin Hokoku 59, 33

4. Adriano, F.T. and Cruz, R. A. (1933). The chemical composition of Philippine mushrooms. Philipp. J. Agric .4, 1-11

5. Food and Agricultural Organization (1972). "Food Composition Table for Use in East Asia." Food Policy and Nutr. Div., Food Agric. Organ. U.N., Rome

Table II Amino Acid Composition of Cultivated and Wild Species of Edible Mushrooms in milligrams of amino acid per gram of corrected crude protein nitrogen.

L. edodes

Protein (% dry wgt)	17.5
Isoleucine	218
Leucine	348
Lysine	174
Methionine	87
Cystine	nd
Phenylalanine	261
Tyrosine	174
Threonine	261
Tryptophan	nd
Valine	261
Argenine	348
Histidine	87
Alanine	305
Aspartic Acid	392
Glutamic Acid	1349
Glycine	218
Proline	218
Serine	261
Total Essential Amino acids	1784
Total Amino acids	4962

Kagawa (1970) Shokuhin Bunseki Hyo

Sawada (1965) Todai Enshurin Hokoku 59, 33

Sugimori, T., Oyama, Y., and Omichi, T. (1971) Studies on basidiomycetes. 1. Productions of mycelium and fruiting body from noncarbohydrate organic substances. J. Ferment. Technol. 49, 435-446

Table III

Vitamin and Mineral Content of Cultivated and Wild Species of Edible Mushrooms in Milligrams per 100 gm of dry weight

Species	Sample	Thia-min	Ribo-flavin	Nia-cin	Ascorbic Acid	Ca	P	Fe	Na	K
L. edodes	Fresh	7.8	4.9	54.9	0	98	476	8.5	61	nd
	Dried	.4	.9	11.9	0	12	171	4.0	19	380

Food and Agricultural Organization (1972). "Food Composition Table for Use in East Asia." Food Policy and Nutr. Div., Food Agric. Organ. U.N., Rome

Absolute Values and Digestibility of the Proteins in Foods (dried material)

	Total protein %	Digestible protein %	Digesti-bility %
Meat	83.7	82.8	98.9
Mushroom*	51.9	45.9	88.5
Spinach	34.5	25.0	72.5
Beans	26.3	23.4	89.0
Rye bread	10.7	9.0	84.1
Potatoes	8.0	7.3	91.2

* The digestibility and absolute values of all protein in mushrooms is relatively high when compared with all foods except meat.

Publications

1. Gray, W.D. *The Use of Fungi as Food and in Food Processing*. Cleveland, Ohio: CRC Press, 1970.

2. Mori, K. *Mushrooms as Health Foods*, Japan: Japan Publ. Inc., 1974.

3. Singer, R. *Mushrooms and Truffles*. New York: Interscience Publ. Inc., 1961.

Appendix 2

Home Cultivation Companies, Kits & Spawn

Mushroompeople, Box 220, Summertown, TN 38483
615-964-2200

Far West Fungi, Box 428, South San Francisco, CA 94083
415-871 0786

Bibliography

Bugialli, Giuliano. *The Fine Art of Italian Cooking*. New York: Times Books, 1977.

Carluccio, Antonio. *A Passion for Mushrooms*. London: Pavilion Books Limited, 1989.

Czarnecki, Jack. *Joe's Book of Mushroom Cookery*. New York: Atheneum, 1986.

Freedman, Louise. *Wild About Mushrooms*. Berkeley: Aris Books, 1987.

Grigson, Jane. *The Mushroom Feast*. New York: Alfred A. Knopf, 1975.

Hazan, Marcella. *The Classic Italian Cook Book*. New York: Alfred A. Knopf, 1980.

Jaffrey, Madhur. *World-of-the-East, Vegetarian Cooking*. New York: Alfred A. Knopf, 1983.

Madison, Debra and Brown, Edward E. *The Greens Cookbook*. New York: Bantam, 1987.

Madison, Deborah. *The Savory Way*. New York: Bantam, June 1990.

Waters, Alice. *Chez Panisse Pasta, Pizza, and Calzone*. New York: Random House, 1984.

Endnotes

1. Ito, T, "Cultivation of Lentinus edodes," in Chang and Hayes (eds), *Biology and Cultivation of Edible Mushrooms*, Academic Press, 1978, p 461.

2. Kuo,D. & Mau Kuo, *How to Grow Forest Mushroom (Shiitake)*, Mushroom Technology Corp, 1983, p 1.

3. Singer, R. and Harris, B., *Mushrooms and Truffles*, Koeltz Scientific Books, Königstein Germany, 1987, p 173.

4. Singer, R., *ibid.*

5. Timmer, Janice, Pershern, Anita, and Ondrus, Marty, "A Nutritional Analysis and Development of Promotional Materials for shiitake Mushroom Producers in Wisconsin," *Shiitake News*, Nov 1990, Lanesboro, MN.

6. Haytowitz, D.B. and Matthews, R.H. (1984) *Composition of Foods: Vegetables and Vegetable Products. Raw, Processed, Prepared.* USDA Agr Handbook No 8-11, Washington DC.

Index

Ask your store to carry our fine line of vegetarian cookbooks

Almost No-Fat Cookbook.....$12.95
Almost No-Fat Holiday Cookbook.....$12.95
Burgers 'n Fries 'n Cinnamon Buns.....$6.95
Chef Neil's International Vegetarian Cooking.....$5.00
Cookin' Healthy with One Foot Out the Door.....$8.95
Cooking with Gluten and Seitan.....$7.95
Delicious Jamaica.....$11.95
Ecological Cooking.....$10.95
Fabulous Beans.....$9.95
From A Traditional Greek Kitchen.....$12.95
From the Global Kitchen.....$11.95
Good Time Eatin' in Cajun Country.....$9.95
Indian Vegetarian Cooking at Your House.....$12.95
Instead of Chicken, Instead of Turkey.....$9.95
Kids Can Cook.....$9.95
Lighten Up! with Louise Hagler.....$11.95
Natural Lunchbox.....$12.95
New Farm Vegetarian Cookbook.....$8.95
Now and Zen Epicure....$17.95
Olive Oil Cookery.....$10.95
The Peaceful Cook.....$8.95
Peaceful Palate.....$15.00
Power of Your Plate.....$10.95
The Shiitake Way.....$9.95
The Shoshoni Cookbook.....$12.95
Solar Cooking.....$8.95
Soyfoods Cookery.....$9.95
The Sprout Garden.....$8.95
Table for Two.....$12.95
Taste of Mexico.....$13.95
Tempeh Cookbook.....$10.95
Tofu Cookery, revised.....$15.95
Tofu Quick & Easy.....$7.95
TVP®Cookbook $6.95
The Uncheese Cookbook.....$11.95
Uprisings: The Whole Grain Bakers' Book....$13.95
Vegetarian Cookbook for People with Diabetes.....$10.95
Vegan Vittles......$11.95

or you may order directly from

Book Publishing Company
P.O. Box 99
Summertown, TN 38483
Please include *2.50 per book* for postage and handling.

1-800-695-2241